Better Regulation in Europe: Netherlands 2010

OECD

ORGANISATION FOR ECONOMIC CO-OPERATION AND DEVELOPMENT

The OECD is a unique forum where the governments of 30 democracies work together to address the economic, social and environmental challenges of globalisation. The OECD is also at the forefront of efforts to understand and to help governments respond to new developments and concerns, such as corporate governance, the information economy and the challenges of an ageing population. The Organisation provides a setting where governments can compare policy experiences, seek answers to common problems, identify good practice and work to co-ordinate domestic and international policies.

The OECD member countries are: Australia, Austria, Belgium, Canada, the Czech Republic, Denmark, Finland, France, Germany, Greece, Hungary, Iceland, Ireland, Italy, Japan, Korea, Luxembourg, Mexico, the Netherlands, New Zealand, Norway, Poland, Portugal, the Slovak Republic, Spain, Sweden, Switzerland, Turkey, the United Kingdom and the United States. The Commission of the European Communities takes part in the work of the OECD.

OECD Publishing disseminates widely the results of the Organisation's statistics gathering and research on economic, social and environmental issues, as well as the conventions, guidelines and standards agreed by its members.

This work is published on the responsibility of the Secretary-General of the OECD. The opinions expressed and arguments employed herein do not necessarily reflect the official views of the OECD or of the governments of its member countries or those of the European Union.

ISBN 978-92-64-08451-3 (print)
ISBN 978-92-64-08456-8 (PDF)

Series: *Better Regulation in Europe*
ISSN 2079-035X (print)
ISSN 2079-0368 (online)

Photo credits: Cover © Ronald Hudson/Fotolia.com

Corrigenda to OECD publications may be found on line at: *www.oecd.org/publishing/corrigenda*.

Foreword

The OECD Review of Better Regulation in the Netherlands is one of a series of country reports launched by the OECD in partnership with the European Commission. The objective is to assess regulatory management capacities in the 15 original member states of the European Union (Austria, Belgium, Denmark, Finland, France, Germany, Greece, Ireland, Italy, Luxembourg, Netherlands, Portugal, Spain, Sweden and the United Kingdom). This includes reviewing trends in their development and identifying gaps in relation to good practice as defined by the OECD and the EU in their guidelines and policies for Better Regulation.

The project is also an opportunity to discuss the follow-up to the OECD's multidisciplinary reviews, for those countries that were part of this process, (Austria, Belgium, Luxembourg and Portugal were not covered by these previous reviews) and to find out what has happened in respect of the recommendations made at the time. The multidisciplinary review of the Netherlands was published in 1999 (OECD (1999), OECD Reviews of Regulatory Reform: Regulatory reform in the Netherlands, OECD, Paris).

The Netherlands was part of the first group to be reviewed – the other three were Denmark, Portugal and the United Kingdom. A second group of countries – Belgium, Finland, France, Germany, Spain and Sweden are expected to be published in the first half of 2010 and the remaining countries will follow in the second half of 2010. This report was discussed and approved for publication at a meeting of the OECD's Working Party on Regulatory Management and Reform on 11 May 2009.

The completed reviews will form the basis for a synthesis report, which will also take into account the experiences of other OECD countries. This will be an opportunity to put the results of the reviews in a broader international perspective, and to flesh out prospects for the next ten years of regulatory reform.

Table of Contents

Figures

Boxes

Tables

Abbreviations and Acronyms

ACTAL	Adviescollege Toetsing Administratieve Lasten – Advisory Board on Administrative Burdens
B4	Beleid voor Burger en Bedrijf – Better Government for Citizens and Businesses
BIA	Business Impact Assessment
BNC	Beoordeling Nieuwe Commissievoorstellen – Working Group for the Assessment of new Commission Proposals
CCD	Common Commencement Dates
CoCo	Co-ordinating Committee
CTW	Commission on Assessing New Legislative Projects
EUPAN	European Public Administration Network
ICER	Interdepartementale Commissie Europees Recht – Interdepartmental Ccommission for European Law
ICRAL	Interdepartmental Commission of Co-ordinators for the Reduction of Administrative Burdens for Citizens
IPAL	Inter-ministerial Unit for Administrative Burdens
IPO	Association of Provinces – Inter Provinciaal Overleg
MDW	Marktwerking, Deregulering en Wetgevingskwaliteit - Market Forces, Deregulation and Legislative Quality
NCA	Netherlands Court of Audit
P&E	Practicability and Enforcement Assessment"
PAL	Programme Administratieve Lastenverlichting – Administrative Burden Reduction Scheme for Citizens
PMO	Prime Minister's Office
REAL	Programme on Regulatory and Administrative Burdens
RIA	Regulatory Impact Assessment
RRG	Regiegroep Regeldruk – Regulatory Reform Group
SER	Social and Economic Council
VNG`	Vereniging van Nederlandse Gemeenten – Association of Netherlands Municipalities

Country Profile – Netherlands

Source: CIA factbook *https://www.cia.gov/library/publications/the-world-factbook/geos/nl.html.*

Country Profile – Netherlands

The land		
Total Area (1000km²):	41	
Agricultural (1000km²):	23	
Major regions/cities (thousand inhabitants, 2006):	Amsterdam Rotterdam The Hague	741 583 476
The people		
Population (thousands):	16 382 (2007)	
Number of inhabitants per sq km:	402 (2007)	
Net increase (2006/2007):	0.2%	
Total labour force (thousands):	8 741 (2007)	
Unemployment rate (% of civilian labour force):	3.5% (2009)	
The economy		
Gross domestic product in USD billion:	676.8	
Per capita (PPP in USD):	41 200	
Exports of goods and services (% of GDP):	73.2% (2006)	
Imports of goods and services (% of GDP):	65.8% (2006)	
Monetary unit:	Euro	
The government		
System of executive power:	Parliamentary	
Type of legislature:	Bicameral	
Date of last general election:	February 2007	
Date of next general election:	9 June 2010	
State structure:	Unitary	
Date of entry into the EU:	Founding member	
Composition of the main chamber (Number of seats):	Christian Democratic Appeal Labour Party (PvdA) Socialist Party Popular Party for Freedom and Democracy Others **Total**	41 32 26 22 29 **150**

Note: 2008 unless otherwise stated

Sources: OECD Economic Survey of the Netherlands 2008, OECD in Figures 2009, OECD Unemployment Outlook 2009, and OECD Government at a Glance 2009.

Executive Summary

Drivers of Better Regulation

The evolution of Dutch economic performance over the last three decades has been closely paralleled by policies aimed at putting Better Regulation on the government's policy agenda, as a means of combating structural and other issues that stood in the way of a stronger growth rate. Regulatory reform gathered momentum through the 1990s, and specific programmes emerged to give regulatory management a clearer shape. The MDW Programme (*Marktwerking, Deregulering en Wetgevingskwaliteit*) was set up in 1994 to improve the regulatory and structural environment for more open markets. Dutch governments at this time sought a new balance between "protection and dynamism", by means of increased competition, regulatory reform and market openness. Pressures to accommodate the emergence of the Single European Market also promoted change. Part of the MDW Programme was to streamline regulations to return to "what is strictly necessary", and this included the reduction of administrative burdens. This was also a decade when significant efforts were made to develop a stronger policy for the development of new regulations, including *ex ante* impact assessment, to avoid the problems of the past.

A second phase started in the late 1990s, with growing emphasis on the reduction of administrative burdens for business. Better Regulation's link with economic performance was re-emphasised in the Coalition Agreement that guides government policy making today, which promotes a more innovative, enterprising and competitive economy. A social aspect has also emerged, partly reflecting the Coalition Agreement's emphasis on social cohesion as well as economic progress, but also as means of supporting public sector reform. Important and emerging aspects of today's Better Regulation policies (such as enforcement, local level Better Regulation, and burdens on citizens) are linked to this broader strategy.

Public governance framework for Better Regulation

The Netherlands is a decentralised unitary state with three tiers of government (central government, provinces and municipalities). The number of municipalities has steadily fallen over time as part of the central government's policy to improve administrative quality and effectiveness through mergers. The central government works on the basis of coalition agreements, which set the policy framework for the four years of the electoral cycle, and annual budget plans. There is an ongoing programme aimed at increasing the efficiency of the civil service, with positive repercussions on aspects of Better Regulation such the streamlining of enforcement practices. The traditional Dutch approach to public governance is based on the corporatist philosophy, which emphasises the principles of consensus building and the use of expert advice to improve regulatory quality, with a view to promoting the legitimacy of regulation and trust in government. Consensus building continues to be an important feature of Dutch governance, but the reforms of the 1990s have also moved the Netherlands towards more open and market driven processes for policy development.

Developments in Better Regulation

Whilst administrative burden reduction has been a key focus of Dutch Better Regulation policy over the last few years, other important policies have also been developed. These include reform programmes for inspection and enforcement, from 2001; programmes to address administrative burdens on citizens which includes elements of regulation inside government, starting in 2003; further work on the legal quality framework for developing new regulations, including assessment of alternatives to regulation; and a growing engagement with the EU institutions over the development of Better Regulation at EU level. Recent developments are extending these foundations. Notably, there is an increasingly vigorous and targeted communication programme, the development of what was previously known as the administrative burden reduction programme, now known as the regulatory burden reduction programme, to cover a much wider scope of issues, moves to strengthen public consultation through the Internet, as well as renewed efforts to work at EU level and with likeminded EU partners to strengthen EU Better Regulation policies.

Main findings of this review

The Netherlands was one of Europe's early starters in the development of Better Regulation policies, and there has been steady progress since the 1990s to build and expand on this. Better Regulation is now on a sustainable track, with successive governments taking initiatives to expand the institutional and policy framework. A range of policies is now in place, alongside the flagship programme to reduce regulatory burdens on business. At this stage, the development of an integrated policy perspective would help to strengthen Dutch Better Regulation by giving it a long term vision and goals.

Institutionally, the establishment of the Regulatory Reform Group, the unit of officials at the centre of government, and of ACTAL, the independent watchdog, have been major milestones in providing a clearer focus for Better Regulation and promoting culture change. The framework is not, however, yet fully complete, as the Regulatory Reform Group only covers business aspects of the Better Regulation agenda. It would be helpful to find a way of further strengthening co-ordination between key ministries. Culture change, as in other OECD countries, still has some way to go.

The Netherlands pioneered the Standard Cost Methodology (SCM) for the reduction of administrative burdens. Achievements for the business sector have been significant, and the 25% net reduction target set by the last cabinet was broadly met. A new 25% reduction target has now been set, and the methodology has been broadened and strengthened. The implementation of this new and even more challenging phase will require sustained attention to the needs of key stakeholders: line ministries, the business community and the parliament. The Netherlands also has a well-developed citizen burden reduction programme, which will require effective monitoring and evaluation.

There is an increasingly urgent need to address *ex ante* impact assessment of new regulations, as current processes do not provide a sufficiently strong framework for a robust, evidence-based development of new regulations. This is an important weakness as it undermines the government's control of new burdens. There appears to be a broad consensus for change. Issues that need attention include the institutional support framework, training and methodologies, the development of an integrated process, and the need to make public consultation an integral part of the process.

There is also a need for rapid improvement of public consultation as an integral part of effective regulatory management. The Netherlands is at cross-roads between longstanding traditions of very structured consultation and the development of new approaches which reach out to stakeholders very differently, not least via the Internet. Improving the approach to consultation does not imply wholesale abandonment of the traditional approaches, but requires to boost transparency and ensure that effective and timely consultation is integral to the development of government policies and in particular to the impact assessment process for new regulations.

The Netherlands is one of the most active participants in the development of EU level Better Regulation strategies. Well-structured processes are in place for the management of EU regulations. The framework is stronger on procedure. Attention is needed to ensure that impacts of EU regulations under development are effectively captured, and on the substantive aspects of transposition of EU regulations into the national context, not least to avoid possible problems of gold plating.

Strategy and policies for Better Regulation

There has been steady progress over a number of years and across successive governments in the development of Better Regulation policies. The Netherlands was one of Europe's pioneers with the development of Better Regulation policies in their own right, starting in the 1980s. Better Regulation has been consciously used to drive important structural changes, economic performance and more recently, to address social and public sector issues. Today, Better Regulation appears to have found a sustainable place in the government's broader policy agenda, reflected in, and providing support for, key elements of the Coalition Agreement. It also engages a growing range of stakeholders – including not just the business community, but also citizens and local levels of government – a factor that will help to secure long-term sustainability.

A range of policies are now in place, alongside the flagship programme to reduce regulatory burdens on business. These include a reform programme for inspection and enforcement, a programme to address administrative burdens on citizens which covers some aspects of regulation inside the administration, further work on the legal quality framework for developing new regulations, including the assessment of alternatives to regulation, and a strong and sustained engagement with the EU institutions over the development of Better Regulation at EU level.

Achievements so far have been significant in the programme to reduce burdens on the business community, and considerable by international standards. This is one of the most longstanding programmes so it is perhaps not surprising, albeit also testimony to effective leadership and management. An updated action plan sets a quantified 25% net reduction target for 2011, additional to the reductions that have already been delivered over the last few years. The policy has been significantly broadened to include other cost factors and quality of regulatory services for businesses. There appears to be no loss of momentum in the inner core of government for driving this policy forward. This, however, is not always reflected elsewhere, with worries about how the latest target will be achieved, and what the substance of the programme should now cover.

Other policies and programmes reflect significant efforts to extend Better Regulation beyond central government and beyond the Netherlands. This includes the new policies and structures for enforcement, the work to support Better Regulation at the EU level and not least the engagement of local levels of government. The Framework Vision Programme for reform of inspections and enforcement appears to be well conceived and advancing steadily. Work to raise consciousness of the need to further develop Better Regulation at the EU level is particularly striking given the relatively small size of the country. Dutch leadership (alongside a small number of other countries) at the EU level is commendable. Considerable effort is also going into developing the interface with local levels of government on Better Regulation.

A significant weakness is the failure so far to implement an effective policy for the *ex ante* impact assessment of new regulations. The weak aspect in Dutch regulatory management today is the absence of any clearly anchored and rigorous process for an evidence-based approach to the development of new regulations. This issue was already picked up in the 2007 OECD report, which noted in effect that whilst the burden reduction programme had been a strong and necessary motor for putting Better Regulation on the map, a broader focus would be needed in the longer term. Fragmentation of the institutional support structure for Better Regulation has not helped.

Two other challenges are apparent, relating to consultation on new regulations and some aspects of EU management. These are the slow progress toward more modern and open forms of consultation for all regulations (not just those which happen to be part of the programmes to reduce burdens on citizens and businesses). The framework for addressing issues of substance arising from EU regulations also needs further attention. Some helpful systems are already in place. The impact of EU regulations on the national market is taken into account in preparing the negotiating position. The Regulatory Reform Group (RRG)'s work includes big efforts to identify and address burdens on business of new EU regulations in the negotiating process. This is helpful but does not address all angles (other stakeholders, the benefits of new regulations). The handling of the transposition of EU-origin regulations remains relatively weak.

The development of an integrated policy perspective including all the elements of a balanced Better Regulation agenda would help to give Dutch Better Regulation a long-term vision. It is beyond the scope of this report to comment on what a longer-term vision might consist of, but we would encourage the Netherlands to start discussing this internally, and with other likeminded countries. Highlighting the links between what is already being done, strengthening the weak parts, and showing how the different elements combine to support and promote high level policy objectives for the economy and society would increase the long-term sustainability of the Better Regulation agenda. It would also demonstrate inclusiveness, by showing that Better Regulation is about new as well as existing regulations, and not (just) about deregulation, nor is it just concerned with the business community. Back in the mid 1990s, the MDW Programme set out a broad vision of Better Regulation and what it could do for public policy goals. The time might be ripe for a "millennium" update. A White Paper could be a useful vehicle for starting the process.

Public communication on Better Regulation is covered by a number of specific strategies and processes. Communication and public documents on Better Regulation tend to be focused on specific programmes. These are essential and need of course to be structured so as to reach their specific target audiences. The most prominent communication strategy is the one established by the RRG for the business burdens reduction programme. The communication policy for the project to reduce administrative burdens on citizens is also well developed. The RRG communication strategy has a broad reach and in some respects acts as the vehicle for communication on overall Better Regulation policy in the Netherlands. As well as the more targeted communication programmes, a more integrated communication of Better Regulation policies might help to highlight the extent of the work carried out, and could also be used as a vehicle for bringing together the different parts of the institutional framework that contribute to Better Regulation.

Many of the programmes are covered by forms of *ex post* evaluation but the approach is not systematic. A number of evaluation processes are in place or under development for specific Better Regulation programmes. *Ad hoc* evaluations also take place and the Netherlands Court of Audit (NCA) has been active. The approach needs to be strengthened in order to ensure that *ex post* evaluation is not overlooked and is an automatic part of all Better Regulation programmes. Internal mechanisms for *ex post* evaluation are also a necessary complement for external evaluations from bodies such as the OECD and the World Bank.

E-Government capacities, a key support for business and citizen burden reduction initiatives, have been steadily developed over time; monitoring and evaluation may need to be boosted. The Netherlands started early, in the 1990s, and has built up a range of projects as well as an institutional framework which reaches out to the local levels of government. A full evaluation of e-government is beyond the scope of this review. However it seems that initiatives to monitor the large number of projects for their practical effectiveness need to be encouraged.

Institutional capacities for Better Regulation

The establishment of the Regulatory Reform Group has been a major step forward in providing a clearer focus for Better Regulation. The merger of several relevant units out of two core and influential ministries (Ministry of Finance and Ministry of Economic Affairs) responsible for the business-related part of Better Regulation policy was the right move. The RRG has established itself as a well known and vigorous Better Regulation entity not only with the business community within the Netherlands, but also across Europe and with the EU institutions. The merger also signals that Better Regulation policy in the Netherlands has reached a certain level of sustainability across coalition and cabinet political cycles, since the RRG is a continuation and strengthening of units set up under previous governments.

The Regulatory Reform Group, however, only covers business aspects of the government's Better Regulation policy. Two other key ministries for Better Regulation are not part of the RRG structure. The Ministry of Justice has long played a critical role in managing the development of new regulations and is currently seeking to develop a new and stronger approach to impact assessment. The Ministry of the Interior and Kingdom Relations is not only responsible for the citizen burden reduction programme, but also has general co-ordinating responsibility for key issues related to Better Regulation (e-Government, general co-ordination of the municipalities and the enforcement inspectorates) and for the civil service (including civil service reform) as well as general relations with the parliament. The Ministry of Foreign Affairs is responsible for important aspects of the general management of EU regulations.

In this context, the establishment of the Steering Group for Better Regulation was a positive move to strengthen links between the key Better Regulation ministries. The group, chaired by the Prime Minister, meets every quarter and brings together the Interior, Justice, Finance and Economic Affairs ministries. It is supported by an officials group. It reviews progress reports on Better Regulation policies and prepares the ground for cabinet and parliamentary reports. The OECD peer review team were told that, from low key beginnings, this group had started to become more proactive, in response to the more controversial phase of reform that the Netherlands now appears to be entering.

The independent watchdog ACTAL is another important institutional asset helping to hold different parts of the agenda together. Since it was established in 2000, the Advisory Board on Administrative Burdens (ACTAL) has played an important role in helping to motivate and structure regulatory reform in the Netherlands (and provided inspiration for other countries to set up similar structures, most recently in Sweden). It is not only important for its challenge function to the government. It also, alongside the Steering Group on Better Regulation, covers several elements of Better Regulation (the business and citizen burden reduction programmes, advice to the Cabinet on the burdens of new regulations which gives it a role in *ex ante* impact assessment, and promotion of Better Regulation at EU level).

An effective institutional framework has also been established for sharing the Better Regulation agenda with the local levels of government. Municipalities have a key interface with business and citizens via their enforcement, planning and licensing responsibilities. The central government agreement with the municipalities and its linked Better Regulation Action Plan provides shape and substance to the roll out of shared Better Regulation goals, such as meeting burden reduction targets.

The central institutional framework for overseeing Better Regulation in its entirety remains, however, relatively weak and fragmented. The Steering Group for Better Regulation, which unites the four main ministries, has so far played an uncertain contribution to the Better Regulation agenda. It does not, for example, appear to have yet played a defining role in promoting the development of a new impact assessment process, which needs a strong central lead to encourage cross ministerial co-operation. This relative fragmentation stands in the way of an even stronger Better Regulation performance. It also means that responsibilities – who does what – are not clear to stakeholders outside the system, and that the system itself does not provide an optimal framework for tackling next steps, notably the development of a stronger impact assessment process. The Ministry of Foreign Affairs, which plays an important role in the management of EU regulations, is not part of the group.

What should be done to strengthen the institutional oversight framework? The radical option would be to expand the RRG's role and structure so that it includes relevant units from other ministries engaged in Better Regulation. However this may not be the most effective way to strengthen co-operation between ministries which each have a strong and distinctive contribution to bring. Short of this option, it is essential that the Steering Group on Better Regulation and its supporting group of officials start to play a more proactive role, based on a well-defined agenda that includes the development of the impact assessment process. In that case, the RRG, as the current main focal point for Better Regulation in the Netherlands, would appear to be best placed to provide the secretariat for the group, perhaps including secondments from other ministries. Strong institutional links between the Ministry of Justice and the other ministries are especially important. The Ministry of Justice is a key player through its role in overseeing legal quality. The 1999 OECD multidisciplinary review on regulatory reform picked up the issue, and the OECD review of the Dutch administrative burden reduction programme picked it up again in 2007.

The need for further support for, and culture change among, implementing ministries needs to be addressed. This is not a new issue (the 1999 OECD report had already noted it), and not unique to the Netherlands. The increasing complexity of the modern reform agenda is a factor. Ministries face a number of challenges for which they need to be well prepared. Stakeholders are more demanding (sometimes both requesting more freedom as well as criticising regulatory failures). The Better Regulation agenda has been broadened to cover the different levels of government. The burden reduction programmes are starting to address more controversial issues. Civil service reforms add a further layer of complexity as well as opportunity (resources are being cut, but this can also be an incentive to update processes). As well as the need for support through enhanced guidance and training, effective carrots and sticks for change need to be in place. The strong link that has been established between showing results for the business burden reduction programme and the budget cycle is helpful. The RRG training and guidance on Better Regulation tools is also important.

The parliament plays a particularly important role in the development of the Better Regulation agenda in the Netherlands. A key player beyond the executive is the parliament. The Dutch political system works on the basis of coalition agreements which set the policy framework for the four years of the electoral cycle. The parliament holds the government closely accountable for implementation of the coalition agreements. It is regularly sent progress reports on different aspects of the Better Regulation programme, and has itself initiated reform of inspections policy. With the extension of the Better Regulation agenda into more difficult and complex territory, its support will be critical.

Transparency through consultation and communication

There is a need for rapid improvement of public consultation as an integral part of effective regulatory management. The Netherlands appears to be at cross-roads between longstanding traditions of very structured consultation (via the search for a consensus through established groups and committees, and the commissioning of expert advice), and the development of new approaches which reach out to stakeholders very differently, not least via the Internet. There is an increasingly urgent need to improve and update the approach to consultation. This does not imply wholesale abandonment of the traditional approaches, but there is a need to boost transparency and ensure that effective and timely consultation is integral to the development of government policies and in particular to the impact assessment process for new regulations. The business and citizen burden reduction programmes have shown the way with new approaches to capture more effectively the real concerns of stakeholders. The pilot project for Internet-based consultation on new regulations across ministries looks very promising.

The introduction of common commencement dates is a very positive step forward. This will put the Netherlands ahead of many other OECD countries. Common commencement dates are fundamentally helpful to business. The presentation to the business community with a set of new regulations "in one shot" may need some management to ensure that it does not (perversely) contribute to poor perceptions of the government's control over the flow of new regulations.

The development of new regulations

Although impact assessment has been established a long time, there is widespread agreement that the current process is in practice unsatisfactory, weak and ineffective. Issues raised in the review included the fact that impact assessment comes too late in the decision-making process to have any effect on outcomes, inadequate consultation, lack of transparency, failure to take into account benefits as well as costs, and the need to define a clear methodological approach balancing qualitative and quantitative analysis. There is an overemphasis on business costs defined fairly narrowly, and an under emphasis on alternatives to regulation (despite the efforts of the Ministry of Justice), benefits, non business impacts, consultation, and on support and quality control, which is fragmented and ineffective. There is little appreciation of the importance of evidence-based, cost-benefit analysis and other methodologies for effective impact assessment. Many of these issues had already been raised in the 1999 OECD report, which drew specific attention to the need for effective quantification, the need to consider alternatives, and the need to consult. There has been progress on some fronts since then, notably the quantification of administrative burdens for business, but not enough to generate an effective approach.

There is concern to control new regulations more effectively. Many stakeholders expressed an underlying concern at the need to control more effectively the burdens that are likely to arise from the flow of new regulations. Some interviewees made the important point that reforming governments – the Netherlands has carried out recent major recent reforms of its health and education sectors – are bound to generate significant new regulation, the effects of which need to be controlled.

At the same time, there does not appear to be a coherent view of how a strengthened impact assessment system might be structured, and no clear vision seems to have emerged from the work of officials to give shape to a new system. For the past two years, a group of officials has been examining ways of improving the process. Despite some useful elements (examining alternatives, web-based consultation) it seems unlikely that these proposals will give rise to an effective, integrated process with real buy-in across government, as the work is mainly promoted by one ministry (Justice) and no clear plan for a new process has yet emerged.

A new approach needs to be developed. The government needs to develop and promote a clear vision and integrated approach to impact assessment, which sets out what impact assessment is for and how it can contribute to stronger, more effective, evidence-based policy making, ensures that new regulations are fit for purpose, and conveys the message that the government understands the importance of bringing new regulations under control. The significant common ground that appears to exist over what is wrong now needs to be translated into a new strategy emphasising the central place that impact assessment has in the policy making process.

Responsibility for carrying out impact assessments should remain with the individual ministries, framed by strong central supervision and quality control. Effective supervision and quality control is crucial to the success of an impact assessment process. The Netherlands rightly emphasise the responsibility of individual ministries. However the current institutional structures for overseeing impact assessments are weak and have fallen into disuse.

Effective training and guidance need to be in place. Officials will need to be trained in the new approach and especially, in the application of the new methodology. The current guidance does not cover cost-benefit analysis or any of the methodologies for quantification. The cultural changes required, particularly in terms of ensuring that senior management is on board, are as important as the development of technical expertise. The recent training on Better Regulation techniques developed by the Ministry of Finance and ACTAL in conjunction with the Ministry of the Interior and Kingdom Relations and the Ministry of Economic Affairs is a positive development.

Methodological rigour is essential and most obviously achieved by cost-benefit analysis, but a quality dimension is equally important. The Netherlands, through its development and promotion of the Standard Cost Model (SCM) for administrative burdens, already has the benefit of a culture that is used to quantitative methods, and quantification is a fundamental pillar for evidence-based policy making. The methodology should therefore have a strong quantitative element, drawing inspiration from the experiences of other OECD countries that are already applying quantification (such as the USA, United Kingdom, Australia). It should also incorporate a strong qualitative aspect, supported by multi-criteria analysis, not least to capture future benefits that may be difficult to monetise. It is important that benefits as well as costs are drawn out, as this is about Better Regulation, not deregulation.

A single integrated, standardised process will help to give impact assessment the focus it needs to be adopted by ministries. Current separate processes need to be integrated into a single process which regroups the different assessments and legal quality tests. This standard process should be adopted across the government. The format for presenting the new integrated impact assessment should be standardised, and kept simple and clear, so that it is comprehensible (the rationale for action and key conclusions of the impact assessment should be readily understood by decision makers as well as other stakeholders including the general public). A staged approach to the process is needed, as now, but institutionally stronger. This would make it clear when, early in the policy development process, impact assessments need to be started, developed and updated, taking account of the need for efforts to be proportional *i.e.* distinguishing between proposals that merit a full impact assessment and others which need less attention. The current process generally only covers primary laws and Orders in Council. Consideration should be given to extending impact assessment to other regulations that are likely to be important for Better Regulation.

Consultation, which is not formally covered at all in the current process, needs to be addressed. Consultation needs to be a formal part of the impact assessment development process and engage all potential stakeholders. Broadly-based consultation (including on the web, building on the Internet pilot for consultation on new regulations that has been launched recently) should start early to give stakeholders the opportunity to comment on proposals before it is too late to influence the outcome, including the possibility of alternatives to regulation. Public consultation on draft impact assessments promotes the sharing of information and expertise, which enriches the draft and encourages ownership.

***Ex post* evaluation also needs to be built into the new process.** Feedback to the government on the effectiveness of the impact assessment process should be built in from the start, as part of the new strategy. There are several options for securing this, which are not mutually exclusive. They include giving ACTAL a role in *ex post* evaluation (building on its role of advice to the Cabinet on regulatory burdens); annual reports to the parliament; tracking the development of new regulations; and last but least, encouraging the Netherlands Court of Audit to carry out audits of the process. Audits by the NCA equivalents in some other countries, notably the United Kingdom, have made an important contribution to evaluating the effectiveness of policies to control the development of new regulations, including impact assessment.

The Ministry of Justice efforts to draw attention to consideration of alternatives to regulation need support and further development, including and not least as part of an enhanced impact assessment process. Regulation may not be the only option. Before it is too late, the process should include consideration of alternative approaches to achieving desired regulatory outcomes. The significant efforts that were started over a decade ago in the use of alternatives need to be given a renewed impetus. The Ministry of Justice has issued a number of relevant documents and these now need to be made operational. An effective approach might examine the consequences of several different options, including an alternative to "command and control" regulation, and the "do nothing" option. Guidance should be developed on the appropriate use of alternatives (such as non-legislative action, exemptions, principles-based rather than rule-based approaches, and outcome standards rather than process standards).

The management and rationalisation of existing regulations

There is no systematic effort to consolidate or simplify the regulatory stock. As in other countries with well developed burden reduction programmes, simplification is mainly a "derivative product" of the efforts to reduce administrative burdens (as for example in the review of regulatory clusters or related laws). As complexity accumulates over time in all areas of regulation, there is a need for more systematic "spring cleaning" at regular intervals. The OECD review team was told that the business community would welcome a "clean-up" of the existing law.

Achievements with the regulatory burden reduction programme have already been considerable by international standards, and the Netherlands' 2003-07 policy identified the main elements of a successful model which has been replicated elsewhere. The 2003-07 Cabinet had a 25% net burden reduction target allocated across ministries, which it broadly achieved. The Dutch model has been an inspiration to other countries, and the considerable investment made by successive Dutch governments since the 1990s has largely paid off. The success factors have been a combination of measurement (the SCM method for the measurement and mapping of burdens); setting a time-bound quantitative target (divided among ministries); a strong inter ministerial co-ordinating unit at the centre of government (the RRG and its predecessor, IPAL); independent monitoring via the watchdog ACTAL; link to the budget cycle; and not least, political support, helped by the narrow focus of the programme on administrative burdens which helped to avoid controversy. It is fair to note that the Netherlands may have had further to go than some other countries, in terms of the relative weight of administrative burdens as a proportion of GDP. But this also means that the Netherlands was probably right to put particular emphasis in the last few years on this part of its Better Regulation strategy.

A new phase has opened up, with the establishment of an ambitious, broad and well-designed new policy. This builds on key elements of the previous policy which have proved their worth (not least a reinforced institutional structure), as well as adding new aspects. The current cabinet has set a further 25% reduction target, based on a (largely) new baseline measurement. The current action plan captures a number of important new issues, as well as addressing weaknesses in the original methodology. This reflects the price paid for being a first mover with no role model to follow, but is also testimony to the fact that the Netherlands is remarkably open to learning from its own and others' experiences, as well as taking advice from independent experts, which it calls in regularly. Among the issues which are being vigorously addressed in this new phase are the extension of the programme to cover burdens at the sub-national levels of government (still very unusual in OECD countries); addressing the burdens raised by enforcement; a renewed attack on the issue of licences; the development of an *ex post* evaluation framework; the establishment of common commencement dates for new regulations; targeting the quality of services related to regulation and not least, the development of the SCM methodology to cover qualitative as well as quantitative aspects and to broaden the definition to cover all compliance costs.

A substantial update and broadening of the programme was necessary, in order to sustain progress towards a new target, but this also raises new challenges. The programme has until recently enjoyed broad support, politically, within ministries, as well as from outside stakeholders. This now looks more vulnerable. As already noted in the 2007 OECD/World Bank report, a politically neutral programme is no longer an option. Proposals for further reform, if they are based on a broader definition of compliance costs, are likely to be politically more sensitive and engage more vested interests. The report also underlined the importance at this stage of having clear goals.

The key stakeholders that matter for progress are: business, implementing ministries, and the parliament. Business is frustrated at what it considers to be slow progress and the failure to tackle issues that really matter from its perspective. There is some discouragement, even resistance, within ministries with regard to the new target, based on a worry that it will not be easy to achieve, as many of the "low hanging fruits" have been cleared off the trees. Even some of the remaining low hanging fruit can raise unexpected problems. The parliament for its part, whilst it takes a keen interest through the regular reports on general progress by the RRG, does not always seem prepared to turn this into specific backing for proposals that require legislative action, without which the new target will not be met.

As regards business, the government is taking the right direction with its expanded definition of compliance costs, and a new communication strategy which is well conceived. For a number of reasons, which are broadly shared with other countries at advanced stages in the deployment of burden reduction programmes, the Netherlands has been confronted with negative business reactions despite evident progress on a number of fronts. The reasons for this include time lags before promised results are delivered; frustration at the scrapping of rules that were not complied with in the first place; and slowness in identifying and addressing key issues for business such as licences delivered by the local level. The situation has not been helped by the redefinition of the baseline for the new target, which calculates that burdens are now only some EUR 10 billion compared with some EUR 16 billion in 2003. The main reason is that information obligations to third parties are no longer part of the definition of administrative burdens, but are now defined as substantive compliance costs. In addition to the administrative burden reduction, the expanded programme has also set targets to reduce these substantive compliance costs. ACTAL underlined to the OECD peer review team that irritants as well as substantive regulatory changes must be addressed at this stage, as businesses do not readily distinguish between administrative burdens and other compliance costs.

The government has reacted comprehensively to the concerns expressed by the business community. As well as the ongoing work to expand the scope of the programme with a methodology that includes irritants and broader compliance costs, and the quality of services, its new highly proactive communications strategy targets needs as identified by business rather than civil servants. This includes the establishment of the *Wientjes Commission* to be the voice of business (which seems to meet with general approval), and a wide range of tailored mechanisms to capture business interests as well as to communicate meaningful achievements (what the recipient wants to know, rather than what the civil servant thinks is interesting). The RRG's communication handbook underlines that concrete results must have been achieved before they are communicated. It is too soon to give a view on the effectiveness of the strategy and regular evaluation will be important, as the government plans to do. The government needs to show results from the new approach fairly quickly if a positive business attitude is to be restored. It plans to evaluate its communications strategy shortly, alongside a "perception monitor survey" this year.

As regards implementing ministries, despite a strong underlying institutional structure, spearheaded by the RRG and ACTAL, there is a need for further support and strengthening of the framework in order to encourage ministries to deliver. The need for enhanced co-operation with "delivery" ministries and further culture change is acknowledged by the RRG. As in other countries, a judicious mix of carrots and sticks is needed. Carrots are important as ministries experiencing fatigue from years of efforts need encouragement. So are sticks, for which sanctions must be credible. The Netherlands has gone further than most other countries in linking achievements to the budget cycle. Consideration should also be given to making a link between achievements and performance appraisals (which would have both a carrot and stick effect). At the same time, ministries need to feel supported in their efforts to push through controversial proposals. This implies some hard choices and trade-offs, for which political support is required. The Cabinet and the Steering Group for Better Regulation chaired by the Prime Minister have an important role to play in this regard.

As regards the parliament, the dialogue needs to be extended to cover specific decisions that will require its approval. The parliament is already heavily engaged in the programme at a strategic level, with the regular reports that it gets from the Cabinet via the *RRG*. There is a need to strengthen and clarify the link between these reports and the specific measures that come to the parliament for approval under the programme. Since the easier targets have been achieved, much of the new work, especially if it is based on an extended interpretation of compliance costs, may need to go through the parliament in order for regulations to be changed or adopted. Skilful piloting will be required. At the same time, although regular updates are essential to sustain parliamentary interest and general support, quarterly reports (even if two of these are short updates) seem excessive, detracting the *RRG* (which prepares the reports) from getting on with the substantive work of developing the programme.

The citizen programme for administrative burden reduction has been carefully developed and adapted to take account of experience in the first phase. The Ministry of the Interior and Kingdom Affairs has developed a programme based on a careful review of what actually matters for citizens. As with the programme for the reduction of burdens on business, from which it was inspired, this project seeks to learn from previous experience (the first phase was acknowledged to be unsatisfactory), to identify the challenges that still need to be met. It makes extensive use of external experts in moving forward. Such openness and willingness to learn is an extremely positive aspect of the Netherlands' general approach to Better Regulation. Among a number of positive features of the project, the local level is engaged in the programme, and extensive use is made of Information and Communication Technologies (ICT). Efforts are made to cover important aspects in the Netherlands geographical context, such as the needs of cross-border workers. Considerable effort goes into promoting an EU level approach to the issues. It is not, however, clear how real progress will be evaluated and measured under an approach which does not set any clear quantitative baseline and reduction target. Without this, it is likely to prove difficult to demonstrate that there have been improvements.

There are considerable and possibly unexploited synergies between the citizen programme and the business burden reduction programme. In a broad sense, the Ministry of the Interior and Kingdom Affairs has learnt from the much longer standing business programme in developing the citizen programme. An element of friendly competition between programmes is also no bad thing. That said, there are numerous points of convergence. These include an overlap in coverage, communication strategy, the use of ICT, a shared independent watchdog (*ACTAL*), and also the development of new qualitative as well quantitative methodologies, some of which might have a shared interest for the two programmes.

Regulation inside government is already part of the citizen programme but could be expanded. Part of the citizen programme addresses regulation inside the administration, notably for professionals working in public services such as hospitals and schools. The aim is to free up time spent on administration so that services to citizens can be enhanced. The Ministry of the Interior and Kingdom Affairs report to the Parliament notes that there is a 25% reduction target for the local levels of government in this respect. Greater emphasis on addressing regulation inside government was already recommended by the 2007

OECD/World Bank report. With a planned cut of 25% in the civil service, development of this part of the programme could help to release resources as well as making a contribution to better service quality.

Compliance, enforcement, appeals

The Netherlands has engaged in pioneer work to ensure that compliance and enforcement are considered at the start of the rule making process. This was already picked up in the 1999 OECD report but deserves to be repeated, in the context of today's interest across the OECD in tackling policy related to the enforcement of regulations as well as their development. Efforts by the Ministry of Justice to raise awareness go back over two decades, via the Directives on Legislation (which it drafts), the legal quality criteria which it applies, and the Practicability and Enforcement Impact Assessment which it also applies. The Netherlands is also responsible for the development of the so-called Table of Eleven determinants of compliance, which have widely influenced other countries' efforts in this field.

There has also been steady development toward a new risk-based approach and structures for enforcement. A well articulated policy which engages the local as well as national levels has been refined through successive cabinets, starting in 2001. Local levels are formally engaged through the central government agreement with municipalities, including pilots for new approaches with a sample of pioneer municipalities.

The establishment of the co-ordinating Inspection Council to promote the new approach has been a successful move and there is close co-operation with the work of the RRG. Is the Ministry of Justice fully engaged? The Council came across to the OECD peer review team as motivated and enthusiastic in its role. There is a close link with the regulatory burden reduction programme for business (reflected in the fact that a reduction of state supervision forms part of the current action plan for the reduction of administrative burdens on business) and close involvement by the RRG in this work. The involvement of the Ministry of Justice, which has played a longstanding upstream role in drawing attention to compliance and enforcement when regulations are developed, is not so clear. Yet the reform programme implies the need to address regulations as they are developed, as much as how they are implemented once adopted.

The current Framework Vision is ambitious as well as quite precise in its goals; careful evaluation of progress is essential if credibility and momentum are to be sustained. The results to date set out in the 2008 report to the parliament appear to be impressive. The report documents for example the establishment of joint risk analyses between inspectorates, co-operation between inspectorates and municipalities, facilities for digital co-operation, and the reassignment of tasks. What has been the real effect of these reforms on the ground? Are these the right targets?

The Ministry of Justice's research report on the state of compliance is a useful initiative to back up further reform. The results should be directly relevant to the further development of the Framework Vision.

The interface between members states and the European Union

Consciousness of the importance of EU origin regulations in shaping the national regulatory environment is high, and the Netherlands are active participants in the development of EU level Better Regulation strategies. For a relatively small country, the Netherlands have been commendably active in raising consciousness of Better Regulation principles at EU level, so that problems are tackled at source, including most recently the importance of effective EU management to keep down burdens on citizens.

Well structured processes are in place for the negotiation and transposition of EU regulations. As in most other EU countries, the Netherlands have developed and established a clear procedural framework for dealing with EU regulations. A particularly strong feature is the process for establishing an implementation plan when an EU regulation is adopted, in which the local levels of government are invited to participate, and the subsequent monitoring of transposition via a centrally co-ordinated database (run by the Ministry of Justice) which systematically tracks and disseminates progress in meeting deadlines for implementation. Transparency as regards the correlation between EU and national regulations is covered under the framework. The processes for ensuring consistency between EU and national regulations (which extend to taking account of the rulings of the European courts) are also noteworthy.

The framework is more effective in securing a sound procedural performance than in addressing issues of substance arising from EU regulations. The EU was a recurring theme across the interviews with the OECD team, with concerns expressed by a number of stakeholders inside and outside government at the difficulties of implementation into the national context. These included a concern about staying up to date with EU developments, with information sometimes being available too late to affect the outcome, and about failures to pay sufficient attention to likely national impacts of EU regulations both at the negotiation and transposition phase of the process. Although the local levels have a formal seat at the committee tables to discuss these matters, the team also heard that more targeted efforts should be made to involve these levels where needed. The most fundamental critique of the current approach was the failure to assess impacts adequately. There is currently no requirement for impact assessment at the negotiation phase, and it is not clear how much is actually done at the transposition phase. The Ministry of Foreign Affairs and the Ministry of Justice lead the various processes, which may leave the framework short of input from other key Better Regulation ministries (Interior, Finance and Economic Affairs).

The interface between subnational and national levels of government

Considerable effort and resources are being put into linking up the local level with national objectives for Better Regulation, and results have started to emerge. There is increasing co-operation between central and local levels of government in key areas of Better Regulation such as reform of inspection practices, the reduction of administrative burdens and licensing reform. Core ministries (Interior, Finance and Economic Affairs) are clearly working hard to involve local governments in their Better Regulation programmes. Central government is providing direct support for municipalities, including consultancy funds to address burden reductions. Concrete results have started to emerge such as the review and simplification of "model regulations" (templates for local regulations produced by the association of municipalities *VNG*), the establishment of a Better Regulation website dedicated to local level Better Regulation issues, and pilot schemes to test the principle of "silence is consent" for licensing.

The central government agreement with the municipalities is an effective means of structuring the approach and identifying priorities. This agreement (under which a specific action plan is drawn up), which is concluded between central government and the VNG at the start of each government term, has been used to good effect to define shared goals.

Uneven progress can be expected and the role of the *VNG* is important for evening out differences across the country. With 443 municipalities (a large number for a relatively small country) and considerable variations in size (and culture), some municipalities are doing better than others. The OECD team were told that progress on licensing reform is especially patchy. The role of the *VNG* is important for disseminating best practice and encouraging horizontal co-operation.

The action plan rightly addresses not only what municipalities can do for central government but also what central government can do for municipalities. The task force for addressing burdens generated by central government (part of the action plan) addresses the important issue of regulatory burdens generated by central government. There is concern at the local level at the weight of new regulations and a desire to see more targeted management of the development of new regulations which will "hit" the local level. The *VNG* has proposed that each ministry appoint a co-ordinating lawyer for new regulation that will affect the local level.

Key recommendations

Strategy and policies for Better Regulation	
1.1	Efforts to engage a wide range of stakeholders beyond the business community should continue to be actively pursued, in the interests of consolidating the broadest possible support base for the future promotion of Better Regulation policies.
1.2	The development of a new policy for the *ex ante* impact assessment of new regulations should be taken forward.
1.3	Efforts should be pursued to strengthen public consultation on new regulations. The overall management of EU regulations should be evaluated with a view to building on the RRG initiatives, and in particular to ensure that transposition of EU – origin regulations is effectively managed.
1.4	Consideration should be given to developing a strategic perspective for the development of Dutch Better Regulation over the longer term.
1.5	As well as the initiatives to communicate on specific programmes, consideration should be given to developing a more integrated communication strategy, so that stakeholders (both within the Netherlands and beyond) can appreciate the complete picture of what is being taken forward, which extends well beyond programmes aimed at the business community.
1.6	Ensure that *ex post* evaluation processes cover all the relevant policies, are systematically applied, and that there is adequate investment in this.

Institutional capacities for Better Regulation	
2.1	The government should consider the best way in which the institutional oversight framework for Better Regulation can be strengthened. The Steering Group on Better Regulation and its supporting group of officials should in any event play a more proactive role, based on a well-defined agenda that includes the development of the impact assessment process.

2.2	The government should review whether incentives for culture change could be strengthened. For example it should review whether the link to the budget cycle for setting targets and assessing performance needs to be given sharper teeth (real consequences for ministerial budgets, effect on the performance appraisal of key officials). Further support for ministries in the shape of guidance and training should also be put in place.
2.3	The government should take active steps to develop a dialogue with relevant parliamentary committees in order to encourage a shared vision of Better Regulation goals and their contribution to wider public policy goals (see also recommendation in Chapter 5 on the business burden reduction programme).

Transparency through public consultation and communication	
3.1	The plans to introduce Internet-based consultation should be pursued, with special attention to accessibility by the general public. Public consultation should be woven into the impact assessment process for new regulations. A code of good practice to be followed by ministries and others with significant responsibilities for new regulations might also be considered.

The development of new regulations	
4.1	The Netherlands should develop a new strategy, structures and processes for the *ex ante* impact assessment of new regulations, taking account of the more detailed proposals set out below.
4.2	A considerably more authoritative form of the Proposed Legislation Desk at official level should be established, reporting directly to the Ministerial Steering Group on Better Regulation chaired by the Prime Minister. This unit, which could be developed on the basis of the current officials' group that supports the Ministerial Steering Group, would have the functions of issuing and updating the relevant guidelines, providing advice and support for ministries in the development of impact assessments, and monitoring the quality of impact assessments, as well as advising ministers directly on the development of the process and the performance of ministries. Consideration should be given to whether the Steering Group should have a formal gatekeeper role for significant new regulatory proposals before they are submitted to the Cabinet (this could be a formal 'sign off", or referral back to the relevant Ministry for more analysis). ACTAL should be considered for an external oversight role, building on its current responsibilities for providing advice to the Cabinet.
4.3	Training should be developed further to cover the overall process and to encourage the development of expertise in evidence-based policy making. There should also be specialised training on applying the methodology, drawing on support from economists as necessary (given that many officials are not economists by training). Methodology should be incorporated into authoritative step-by-step guidance for officials, which should also make clear the responsibilities of the various decision makers through the process (ministers, officials, the ministerial Steering Group, the supporting officials' group, officials themselves).

4.4	A clear methodology with a quantity/quality balance should be established.
4.5	Establish a single integrated process for impact assessment across government, which includes a simple format, the stages of the process with the emphasis on starting early, and a clear and comprehensive definition of the regulations covered.
4.6	Ensure that the EU and local dimensions are effectively covered in the new process.
4.7	Impact assessment reports should be published on ministry websites, as well as the website of the lead supervisory authority, both at an appropriate drafting stage, and when finalised. Those who have contributed to consultation should be advised of the impact assessment's publication, and where important comments have been made, given feedback on how the comments were used (or an explanation of why they were not used). The views of the external oversight body should also be made public. Efforts should be made to ensure that the non-business community (those who may not have such as strong voice such as citizens and consumer advocacy bodies) are engaged with the process.
4.8	Consideration should be given to the best way of arranging systematic *ex post* evaluation of the impact assessment process. The Ministry of Justice should be encouraged in its work to track the trends in development of new regulations.
4.9	As already recommended in the 1999 OECD report, the consideration of alternatives needs to be clearly and firmly anchored into a revitalised impact assessment process.

The management and rationalisation of existing regulations	
5.1	The government should evaluate regularly the effectiveness and results of its action plan and communication strategy (as it plans to do).
5.2	The government should ensure that budgetary and performance sanctions (or rewards) are in place and are credible, to encourage meeting of targets. The Steering Group for Better Regulation needs to play a strong role in dealing with the more controversial proposals that will arise, settling trade-offs and providing collective political support under the aegis of the Prime Minister for the adoption of such proposals
5.3	The government should reduce the number of reports made to the parliament on the programme, from quarterly to half yearly, without reducing their substantive content. It should balance reporting with a consideration of how to strengthen the dialogue with key parliamentary committees in order to encourage a positive attitude to proposals for change under the programme. The RRG should also, as far as possible, encourage ministries to link related proposals into packages before they are put to the parliament, drawing attention to their contribution (where appropriate) to the main strategic objectives of the programme.
5.4	The government should consider how it can best give shape to a concrete target or targets, linked to a clear baseline that would enable stakeholders to assess progress.
5.5	The government should consider whether it would be helpful to reinforce links between the different programmes, and ensure that areas of common interest are addressed jointly.

5.6	Consideration should be given to expanding the elements of the project that address regulation inside government.

Compliance, enforcement, appeals	
6.1	The government should consider how it can share experiences and ideas on more effective enforcement with other countries, both to learn from them and to disseminate its own successes.
6.2	The Ministry of Justice needs to be fully engaged in developing the programme, especially as the current Framework Vision seeks to promote a fundamental reform of attitudes to underlying rules and policy.
6.3	Steps should be taken to ensure that regular and independent evaluations are carried of the results emerging from the Framework Vision.

The interface between member states and the European Union	
7.1	The government should carry out a review of current processes for the negotiation and transposition of EU regulations, in order to map strengths and weaknesses, to deepen the involvement of the Interior, Finance and Economic Affairs ministries, and to strengthen procedures and guidance aimed at addressing substantive issues. Impact assessment of EU regulations both at the negotiation and transposition phase should be made a formal requirement and an integral part of the new impact assessment process.

The interface between subnational and national levels of government	
8.1	Further development of the shared agenda for Better Regulation should pay particular attention to licensing, and to finding effective ways of addressing the likely impact of centrally generated regulations on the local level. This issue should be included in the proposed review of *ex ante* impact assessment.

Introduction: Conduct of the review

Peer review and country contributions

The review was conducted by a team consisting of members of the OECD Secretariat, and peer reviewers drawn from the administrations of other European countries with expertise in Better Regulation. The review team for the Netherlands was:

- Caroline Varley, Project Leader for the EU15 reviews, Regulatory Policy Division of the Public Governance Directorate, OECD.
- Andrew van der Lem, Director and Head of International (Europe) Team, Better Regulation Executive, Department for Business, Enterprise, and Regulatory Reform, United Kingdom.
- Tríona Quill, Head of Better Regulation Unit, Department of the Taoiseach (Prime Minister), Ireland.

The review team held discussions in The Hague with Dutch officials and external stakeholders on 26 March 2008 and 13-16 April 2008. Major initiatives and developments between these missions and clearance of the report for publication in May 2009 are referenced, but have not been evaluated.

The team interviewed representatives of the following organisations:

- Advisory Board on Administrative Burdens (ACTAL)
- Association of Netherlands Municipalities (VNG)
- Business and Policy Research Institute (EIM)
- Central Unit for Modernising Inspections
- Confederation of Netherlands Industry and Employers (VNO-NCW)
- Erasmus University (Faculty of Social Sciences)
- General Inspection Service
- House of Representatives
- Ministry of Agriculture
- Ministry of Economic Affairs
- Ministry of Finance
- Ministry of Foreign Affairs
- Ministry of General Affairs (Prime Minister's Office)
- Ministry of Interior and Kingdom Relations
- Ministry of Justice
- Ministry of Social Affairs and Employment
- Municipality of Amsterdam
- Netherlands Court of Audit (NCA)
- Prime Minister's Office
- Regulatory Reform Group
- Transport and Water Management Inspectorate
- *Wientjes* Commission

Within the OECD Secretariat, the EU 15 project is led by Caroline Varley, supported by Sophie Bismut. Elsa Cruz de Cisneros and Shayne MacLachlan provided administrative and communications support, respectively, for the development and publication of the report.

Structure of the report

The report is structured into eight chapters. The project baseline is set out at the start of each chapter. This is followed by an assessment and recommendations, and background material.

- *Strategy and policies for Better Regulation.* This chapter first considers the drivers of Better Regulation policies and the country's public governance framework seeks to provide a "helicopter view" of Better Regulation strategy and policies. It then considers overall communication to stakeholders on strategy and policies, as a means of encouraging their ongoing support. It reviews the mechanisms in place for the evaluation of strategy and policies aimed at testing their effectiveness. Finally, it (briefly) considers the role of e-Government in support of Better Regulation.

- *Institutional capacities for Better Regulation.* This chapter seeks to map and understand the different and often interlocking roles of the entities involved in regulatory management and the promotion and implementation of Better Regulation policies. It also examines training and capacity building within government.

- *Transparency through consultation and communication.* This chapter examines how the country secures transparency in the regulatory environment, both through public consultation in the process of rule- making and public communication on regulatory requirements.

- *The development of new regulations.* This chapter considers the processes, which may be interwoven, for the development of new regulations: procedures for the development of new regulations (forward planning; administrative procedures, legal quality); the *ex ante* impact assessment of new regulations; and the consideration of alternatives to regulation.

- *The management and rationalisation of existing regulations.* This chapter looks at regulatory policies focused on the management of the "stock" of regulations. These policies include initiatives to simplify the existing stock of regulations, and initiatives to reduce burdens which administrative requirements impose on businesses, citizens and the administration itself.

- *Compliance, enforcement, appeals.* This chapter considers the processes for ensuring compliance and enforcement of regulations, as well administrative and judicial review procedures available to citizens and businesses for raising issues related to the rules that bind them.

- *The interface between the national level and the European Commission.* This chapter considers the processes that are in place to manage the negotiation of EU regulations, and their transposition into national regulations. It also briefly considers the interface of national Better Regulation policies with Better Regulation policies implemented at EU level.

- *The interface between sub national and national levels of government.* This chapter considers the rule-making and rule-enforcement activities of local / sub-federal levels of government, and their interplay with the national / federal level. It reviews the allocation of regulatory responsibilities at the different levels of government, the capacities of the local / sub-federal levels to produce quality regulation, and co-ordination mechanisms between the different levels.

Methodology

The starting point for the reviews is a "project baseline" which draws on the initiatives for Better Regulation promoted by both the OECD and the European Commission over the last few years:

- The OECD's 2005 Guiding Principles for Regulatory Quality and Performance set out core principles of effective regulatory management which have been tested and debated in the OECD membership.
- The OECD's multidisciplinary reviews over the last few years of regulatory reform in 11 of the 15 countries to be reviewed in this project included a comprehensive analysis of regulatory management in those countries, and recommendations.
- The OECD/SIGMA regulatory management reviews in the 12 "new" EU member states carried out between 2005 and 2007.
- The 2005 renewed Lisbon Strategy adopted by the European Council which emphasises actions for growth and jobs, enhanced productivity and competitiveness, including measures to improve the regulatory environment for businesses. The Lisbon Agenda includes national reform programmes to be carried out by member states.
- The European Commission's 2006 Better Regulation Strategy, and associated guidelines, which puts special emphasis on businesses and especially SMEs, drawing attention to the need for a reduction in administrative burdens.
- The European Commission's follow up Action Programme for reducing administrative burdens, endorsed by the European Council in March 2007.
- The European Commission's development of its own strategy and tools for Better Regulation, notably the establishment of an impact assessment process applied to the development of its own regulations.
- The OECD's recent studies of specific aspects of regulatory management, notably on cutting red tape and e-Government, including country reviews on these issues.

The report, which was drafted by the OECD Secretariat, was the subject of comments and contributions from the peer reviewers as well as from colleagues within the OECD Secretariat. It was fact checked by the Netherlands.

The report is also based on material provided by the Netherlands in response to a questionnaire, including relevant documents, as well as relevant recent reports and reviews carried out by the OECD and other international organisations on linked issues such as e-Government and public governance.

Regulation: What the term means for this project

The term "regulation" in this project is generally used to cover any instrument by which governments set requirements on citizens and enterprises. It therefore includes all laws (primary and secondary), formal and informal orders, subordinate rules, administrative formalities and rules issued by non-governmental or self-regulatory bodies to whom governments have delegated regulatory powers. The term is not to be confused with EU regulations. These are one of three types of EC binding legal instrument under the Treaties (the other two being directives and decisions).

Chapter 1

Strategy and policies for Better Regulation

Regulatory policy may be defined broadly as an explicit, dynamic, and consistent "whole-of-government" policy to pursue high-quality regulation. A key part of the OECD's 2005 Guiding Principles for Regulatory Quality and Performance is that countries adopt broad programmes of regulatory reform that establish principles of "good regulation", as well as a framework for implementation. Experience across the OECD suggests that an effective regulatory policy should be adopted at the highest political levels, contain explicit and measurable regulatory quality standards, and provide for continued regulatory management capacity.

Effective communication to stakeholders is of growing importance to secure ongoing support for regulatory quality work. A key issue relates to stakeholders' perceptions of regulatory achievements, and how progress can be effectively communicated (business, for example, may continue to complain about regulatory issues that are better managed than previously).

Governments are accountable for the often significant resources as well as political capital invested in regulatory management systems. There is a growing interest in the systematic evaluation of regulatory management performance – "measuring the gap" between regulatory policies as set out in principle and their efficiency and effectiveness in practice. How do specific institutions, tools and processes perform? What contributes to their effective design? The systematic application of *ex post* evaluation and measurement techniques can provide part of the answer and help to strengthen the framework.

E-Government is an important support tool for Better Regulation. It permeates virtually all aspects of regulatory policy from consultation and communication to stakeholders, to the effective development of strategies addressing administrative burdens, and not least as a means of disseminating Better Regulation policies, best practices, and guidance across government, including local levels. Whilst a full evaluation of this aspect is beyond the scope of this exercise and would be inappropriate, the report makes a few comments that may prove helpful for a more in depth analysis.

Assessment and recommendations

Development of Better Regulation strategy and policies

There has been steady progress over a number of years and across successive governments in the development of Better Regulation policies. The Netherlands was one of Europe's pioneers with the development of Better Regulation policies in their own right, starting in the 1980s. Better Regulation has been consciously used to drive important structural changes, economic performance and more recently, to address social and public sector issues. Today, Better Regulation appears to have found a sustainable place in the government's broader policy agenda, reflected in, and providing support for, key elements of the Coalition Agreement. It also engages a growing range of stakeholders – including not just the business community, but also citizens, and local levels of government – a factor that will help to secure long-term sustainability.

Recommendation 1.1. Efforts to engage a wide range of stakeholders beyond the business community should continue to be actively pursued, in the interests of consolidating the broadest possible support base for the future promotion of Better Regulation policies.

A range of policies are now in place, alongside the flagship programme to reduce regulatory burdens on business. These include a reform programme for inspection and enforcement, a programme to address administrative burdens on citizens and regulation inside the administration, further work on the legal quality framework for developing new regulations, including the assessment of alternatives to regulation, and a strong and sustained engagement with the EU institutions over the development of Better Regulation at EU level.

Achievements so far have been significant in the programme to reduce burdens on the business community, and considerable by international standards. This is one of the most longstanding programmes so it is perhaps not surprising, albeit also testimony to effective leadership and management. An updated action plan sets a quantified 25% net reduction target for 2011, additional to the reductions that have already been delivered over the last few years. The policy has been significantly broadened to include other cost factors and quality of regulatory services for businesses. There appears to be no loss of momentum in the inner core of government for driving this policy forward. This, however, is not always reflected elsewhere, with worries about how the latest target will be achieved, and what the substance of the programme should now cover.

Other policies and programmes reflect significant efforts to extend Better Regulation beyond central government and beyond the Netherlands. These include new policies and structures for enforcement, the work to support Better Regulation at the EU level, and not least the engagement of local levels of government. The Framework Vision Programme for reform of inspections and enforcement appears to be well conceived and advancing steadily. Work to raise consciousness of the need to further develop Better Regulation at the EU level is particularly striking given the relatively small size of the country. Dutch leadership (alongside a small number of other countries) at the EU level is commendable. Considerable effort is also going into developing the interface with local levels of government on Better Regulation.

A significant weakness is the failure so far to implement an effective policy for the ex ante impact assessment of new regulations. The "poor relation" in Dutch regulatory management today is the absence of any clearly anchored and rigorous process for an evidence based approach to the development of new regulations. This issue was already picked up in the 2007 OECD report on administrative simplification, which noted in effect that whilst the burden reduction programme had been a strong and necessary motor for putting Better Regulation on the map, a broader focus would be needed in the longer term.[1] Fragmentation of the institutional structure (addressed in the next chapter) has not helped.

Box 1.1. Comments from the 2007 OECD report on Administrative Simplification in the Netherlands: The balance of the Dutch Better Regulation strategy

The Netherlands have been a main driver in the trend towards more evidence-based programmes to reduce administrative burdens on companies and was among the first to launch a 25% burden reduction programme. A similar exercise has been undertaken to reduce administrative burdens on citizens. In both domains, the Netherlands is seen as a front-runner and has inspired other countries.

The linkage between the burden reduction programme and other programmes and initiatives for public sector modernisation and reform is (however) rather weak. This may lead to a loss of possible synergies and difficulties of co-ordination and communication. The e-Government programme is an example of a related programme with a high correspondence in goals, tools and target groups, which has not been linked to the programme for the reduction of administrative burdens. Problems of co-ordination are also seen in the relationship between central and local governments, the relationship between ministries, and programmes seem to have been suffering from a lack of integration.

Recommendation 1.2. The development of a new policy for the *ex ante* impact assessment of new regulations should be taken forward (Chapter 4 gives more detail).

Two other challenges are apparent, relating to consultation on new regulations and some aspects of EU management. These are the slow progress toward more modern and open forms of consultation for all regulations (not just those which happen to be part of the programmes to reduce burdens on citizens and businesses). The framework for addressing issues of substance arising from EU regulations also needs further attention. Some helpful systems are already in place. The impact of EU regulations on the national market is taken into account in preparing the negotiating position. The Regulatory Reform Group (RRG)'s work to address substantial regulatory burdens on business arising from EU regulations includes big efforts to identify and address these in the negotiating process (see Chapter 8). This is helpful but does not address all angles (other stakeholders, the benefits of new regulations). The handling of the transposition of EU-origin regulations remains weak.

Recommendation 1.3. Efforts should be pursued to strengthen public consultation on new regulations. The overall management of EU regulations should be evaluated with a view to building on the RRG initiatives, and in particular to ensure that transposition of EU – origin regulations is effectively managed.

The development of an integrated policy perspective including all the elements of a balanced Better Regulation agenda would help to give Dutch Better Regulation a long-term perspective and vision. It is beyond the scope of this report to comment on what a longer term vision might consist of, but we would encourage the Netherlands to start discussing this internally, and with other likeminded countries. Highlighting the links between what is already being done, strengthening the weak parts, and showing how the different elements combine to support and promote high-level policy objectives for the economy and society would increase the long-term sustainability of the Better Regulation agenda. It would also demonstrate inclusiveness, by showing that Better Regulation is about new as well as existing regulations, and not (just) about deregulation, nor is it just concerned with the business community. Back in the mid 1990s, the *MDW* programme set out a broad vision of Better Regulation and what it could do for public policy goals. The time might be ripe for a "millennium" update. A white paper could be a useful vehicle for starting the process.

Recommendation 1.4. Consideration should be given to developing a strategic perspective for the development of Dutch Better Regulation over the longer term.

Communication on Better Regulation strategy and policies

Public communication on Better Regulation is covered by a number of specific strategies and processes. Communication and public documents on Better Regulation tend to be focused on specific programmes. These are essential and need of course to be structured so as to reach their specific target audiences. The most prominent communication strategy is the one established by the RRG for the business burdens reduction programme. The communication policy for the project to reduce administrative burdens on citizens is also well developed. The RRG communication strategy has a broad reach and in some respects acts as the vehicle for communication on overall Better Regulation policy in the Netherlands. Some aspects of policy could, however, be given greater prominence, for example the important new policies on enforcement. As well as the more targeted communication programmes, a more integrated communication of Better Regulation policies might help to highlight the extent of the work carried out, and could also be used as a vehicle for bringing together the different parts of the institutional framework that contribute to Better Regulation.

Recommendation 1.5. As well as the initiatives to communicate on specific programmes, consideration should be given to developing a more integrated communication strategy, so that stakeholders (both within the Netherlands and beyond) can appreciate the complete picture of what is being taken forward, which extends well beyond programmes aimed at the business community.

Ex post evaluation of Better Regulation strategy and policies

Many of the programmes are covered by forms of ex post evaluation but the approach is not systematic. A number of evaluation processes are in place or under development for specific Better Regulation programmes. *Ad hoc* evaluations also take place and the Netherlands Court of Audit has been active. The approach needs to be strengthened in order to ensure that *ex post* evaluation is not overlooked and is an automatic part of all Better Regulation programmes. Internal mechanisms for *ex post* evaluation are also a necessary complement for external evaluations from bodies such as the OECD and the World Bank.[2]

Recommendation 1.6. Ensure that *ex post* evaluation processes cover all the relevant policies, are systematically applied, and that there is adequate investment in this.

E-Government in support of Better Regulation

E-Government capacities, a key support for business and citizen burden reduction initiatives, have been steadily developed over time; monitoring and evaluation may need to be boosted. The Netherlands started early, in the 1990s, and has built up a range of projects as well as an institutional framework which reaches out to the local levels of government. A full evaluation of e-Government is beyond the scope of this review. However it seems that initiatives to monitor the large number of projects for their practical effectiveness need to be encouraged.

Background

Economic context and drivers of Better Regulation

The evolution of Dutch economic performance over the last three decades has been closely paralleled by policies aimed at putting Better Regulation on the government's policy agenda, as a means of combating structural and other issues that stood in the way of a stronger growth rate.[3]

The real start of Better Regulation was triggered when the Netherlands faced a severe economic crisis in the 1980s. This forced a wide ranging stock taking of post-war economic policies and the corporatist system of public governance, under which the state shared public policy development with organised labour and business. The system had developed rigidities and the dominating role of insiders, often reflecting producer interests in protected markets, made it difficult to encourage economic development based on more open and competitive markets. The regulatory framework reflected this, with complexities that had accumulated over time from efforts to accommodate interest groups, a lack of transparency and slow decision making arising from the constant search for consensus.

Various commissions and reports from the mid 1980s onward drew attention to these issues, culminating in the launch of the so called *MDW* programme (*Marktwerking, Deregulering en Wetgevingskwaliteit* – Market Forces, Deregulation and Legislative Quality) in 1994 which sought to improve the regulatory and structural environment for more open markets. Dutch governments at this time sought a new balance between "protection and dynamism", by means of increased competition, regulatory reform and market openness. Pressures to accommodate the emergence of the Single European Market also promoted change.

Regulatory reform gathered momentum through the 1990s, and specific programmes emerged to give the new regulatory management a clearer shape. Part of the *MDW* programme was to streamline regulations to return to "what is strictly necessary", and this included the reduction of administrative burdens. In 1993 it was estimated that the aggregate costs of administrative burdens on companies was more than 2% of GDP. This was also a decade when significant efforts were made to develop a stronger policy for the development of new regulations, including *ex ante* impact assessment, to avoid the problems of the past.

A second phase can be identified starting in the late 1990s, with growing emphasis on the reduction of administrative burdens for business, which was given policy shape through increasingly detailed and wide ranging programmes based on quantification of the burdens and of targets for reduction. Better Regulation's link with economic performance was re-emphasised in the Coalition Agreement that guides government policy making today, which emphasises the promotion of a more innovative, enterprising and competitive economy.

A social aspect has also emerged, partly reflecting the Coalition Agreement's emphasis on social cohesion as well as economic progress, but also as means of supporting public sector reform. The 2003 government launched a major programme for public sector reform, consisting of four action lines: the government will improve its services to citizens; the government will regulate less, and differently; central government will organise itself better; and the government will reform its relations with the local levels of government.[4] Important and emerging aspects of today's Better Regulation policies (such as enforcement, local level Better Regulation, and burdens on citizens) are linked to this broader strategy.

Main developments in the Netherlands Better Regulation agenda

The main staging posts are set out in Table 1.1. The Netherlands was a pioneer in the development of Better Regulation as a distinct policy field, and Dutch regulatory policy goes back a long way, starting in 1984 with a wide ranging report on the (then) weaknesses of the Dutch administrative and legal system. Various efforts were made over the next ten years to address the issues raised, including a tightening up of processes for the development of new regulations and the introduction of an impact assessment process. The next major milestone was the 1994 *MDW* programme which drew attention to the need for better functioning of markets, the importance of legislative quality, and the need for deregulation, including not least the need to set up a programme to reduce burdens on business.

This marked an important strategic swing toward administrative burden reduction as the main (though not the only focus) of Dutch Better Regulation policy. The *Slechte* Committee in 1998 further emphasised the importance of administrative burdens, and laid the groundwork for today's approach, setting in motion a succession of increasingly focused action plans for business burden reduction.

The last few years, however, have also seen the development of other important policies. These include reform programmes for inspection and enforcement, from 2001; the programmes to address administrative burdens on citizens and burdens of regulation inside government, started in 2003; further work on the legal quality framework for developing new regulations, including assessment of alternatives to regulation; and a growing engagement with the EU institutions over the development of Better Regulation at EU level.

Generally, as in some other OECD countries, it can be said that Better Regulation has finally emerged as a strong policy field in its own right.

Table 1.1. Milestones in the development of Better Regulation policies in the Netherlands

1984	*Geelhoed* Commission report argues that the corporatist elements of the Dutch administrative and legal system bear major responsibility for an excessively complex, onerous and overbearing regulatory structure. The directives on legislation (rules for the development of regulations are expanded to include a wider range of legislative quality issues not only related to technical law-drafting.
1985	*Grapperhaus* Commission report on compliance costs and proposes further reforms, including the introduction of a requirement for regulatory impact assessment. Council of State identifies major regulatory quality issues that need to be addressed including institutional law / policy-making relationships, inter-ministerial co-ordination and the recruitment and development of law-drafting experts.
1987	Commission on Assessing New Legislative Projects (CTW).
1991-92	Quality framework to guide the development of new regulations is established. Directives on legislation are further revised.
1993	General Accounting Office completes review of regulatory processes, concluding that most of the problems identified by the Council of State in 1985 were still unsolved.
1994	Launch of *MDW* programme (*Marktwerking, Deregulering en Wetgevingskwaliteit*), which becomes a formal part of the government's overall policy programme. This targets the functioning of markets, deregulation and legislative quality. One of the aims was to streamline regulations to return to "what is strictly necessary", leading to the first programmes aimed at reducing administrative burdens. The programme also led to an overhaul of regulatory impact

	assessment requirements. *Van Lunteren* Commission examines taxation on SMEs and new enterprises.
1998-99	New coalition agreement establishes "*MDW* 2". *Slechte* Committee report presents 60 projects for the reduction of administrative burdens on business, and confirms the business focus of the programme, as well as the adoption of a narrow definition of compliance costs (to depoliticise the programme).
2001	Launch of the first formal reform programme (Framework Vision) for inspection and enforcement, following the Enschede fireworks disaster.
2003	Launch of a major programme for public sector reform (*Andere Overheid – A Different Government*) following the election. This consisted of four major action lines: the government will improve its provision of services to citizens; it will regulate less, and differently; central government will organise itself better; central government will reform its relations with local municipalities and provinces. Within this context, launch of the first citizens' administrative burden reduction programme and development of an action plan for the reduction of administrative burdens at local level.
2003	Launch of the administrative burden reduction programme for businesses
2005	Launch of the programme to simplify permits (including *lex silencio* – silence is consent) Launch of the second Framework Vision for inspection and enforcement.
2004	Dutch EU Presidency: high-level political prioritisation of the economic character of Better Regulation on the EU agenda, with a strong emphasis on administrative burdens for businesses in particular. Several initiatives are developed, such as the conference "Simple is better", the *EcoFin* paper "Fostering economic growth by reducing administrative burdens for businesses in the EU" and the co-ordination of 300 simplification proposals for the EU administrative simplification programme. The Netherlands, in co-operation with other EU presidencies, also promotes long-term planning of the Better Regulation Agenda by agreeing on priorities and policies with four – later expanded to six – consecutive presidencies.
2007	Following the election, establishment of a revised and expanded action plan for business administrative burdens, a revised programme for reduction of burdens on citizens, professionals and inter-governmental burdens, and an updated Framework Vision for inspections and enforcement. Further development of the action plan for the reduction of administrative burdens at local level.

Source: Dutch government.

Guiding principles for Better Regulation

As for most other OECD countries, there is no single strategy document that currently sets out the entirety of the Dutch Better Regulation agenda. The context for the different elements of the agenda can be found by reference to the broader framework of government policies reflected in the Coalition Agreement. This emphasises (among other issues) public sector reform aimed at a smaller and more efficient central government, the promotion of a more innovative, enterprising and competitive economy, and an active role in Europe and beyond. Specific strategy papers frame each element of the Better Regulation agenda. These include for example the Framework Vision for inspection and supervision, and not least, the Regulatory Reform Group's White Paper setting out the current action plan for the reduction of regulatory burdens on business.

Following the November 2006 election, a Cabinet White Paper set the scene for a substantial broadening and update of the programme for the reduction of administrative burdens on businesses. The broader scope of the new programme is reflected in the fact that reference is now to "regulatory" burdens on businesses (*i.e.* not only administrative burdens). The policy also includes a local level dimension via improvement in the level of service by municipalities. It also provides for a reduction in the supervisory costs of inspections, aimed at promoting a more efficient, flexible, user-friendly and risk-based approach to enforcement.

Main Better Regulation policies

The reduction of regulatory burdens on businesses remains the focal point of the current agenda. The 2007-2011 programme adopted by the Cabinet after the last election is structured around three principles which it has defined as:

- *Less* annoyance for businesses from things that irritate them.
- Make things *simpler* for business – for instance, with faster and better service.
- Ultimately, by decreasing the regulatory burden and making it easier for businesses to comply with the obligations imposed by government, there will be less regulatory burden in the *perception* of business.

These principles have been given effect in the June 2007 Regulatory Burden Action Plan via concrete "3x4 objectives" of "Less, Simpler and Tangible", which yield twelve indicators against which progress will be measured, and which will be the subject of integrated reports on a regular basis through to 2011 (the end of the current Cabinet term of office). The objectives are:

- A quantitative 25% net reduction target for 2011 for administrative burdens on business, additional to the reductions that have already been achieved under previous programmes.
- Reduction in regulatory compliance costs, where they are disproportionately high for business relative to the public interest served by the regulations.
- Reduction in the costs of supervision across selected domains (after consultation with business representatives), the aim being an average of 25% in each domain.
- Reduction in the management and implementation costs of all existing national government subsidies to business, while continuing to guarantee their legitimacy.
- Acceleration of procedures for the issue of permits, by combining permits and, where possible, by the greater use of *lex silencio* (silence is consent).
- Faster and better services to business, by improving the professionalism and client orientation of services provided by the government.
- Improvement in the provision of information to business, as far as possible through a single channel, with the introduction of common commencement dates for new regulations and readable forms.

The Netherlands Better Regulation agenda also includes the following aspects:

- *Improved law making and impact assessment of new regulations.* Policies for impact assessment of new regulations have been in place for many years, closely linked to, and overlapping with, a wide ranging framework for promoting legal quality, including the use of alternatives and attention to downstream compliance and enforcement. Efforts are currently being made to develop a stronger and more integrated impact assessment policy.

- *Reduction of administrative burdens for citizens, reduction of regulation inside government and reduction of inter-governmental burdens.* A revised programme is in place following the last elections. This is based on a qualitative approach, with the identification of the "top ten" most irritating burdens for citizens and the development of "life analysis" (to pinpoint the administrative issues that different categories of citizen are confronted with in the bureaucracy. A part of this programme addresses regulation inside the administration, notably for professionals in public services such as hospitals and schools, and between levels of government.

- *Local governments.* An Action Plan for the reduction of administrative burdens at local level links up central government and the municipalities in a shared effort to address, in particular, administrative burdens, and to promote best practices.

- *EU level Better Regulation.* An important part of the policies addressing burdens on business and citizens in the Netherlands is a sustained effort (in tandem with other likeminded EU countries) to encourage progress at EU level, where an increasing number of regulations are developed.

- *Consultation on new regulations.* A policy to boost transparency and consistency of consultation approaches on the development of new regulations, via the Internet, is under development.

Communication on the Better Regulation agenda

Reflecting the fact that there is no single overarching Better Regulation strategy document (apart from the very broad-based Coalition Agreement, which is presented to the general public), as well as the need for tailored approaches to each programme, public communication on Better Regulation is covered by a number of specific strategies and processes. Regular reports to the parliament are made on the main programmes and these are posted on the parliament's website. Reports are also available on the government's website[5] and circulated directly to stakeholder networks.

The most prominent communication strategy is the one established by the Regulatory Reform Group to convey and discuss developments in the programme to reduce administrative burdens on business. This to some extent (because it does not cover all the initiatives, and the main target stakeholders are businesses) acts as a general focal point for informing stakeholders about Better Regulation. The RRG's communication strategy is based on a broad public relations framework, as well as business sector specific communication. Business "ambassadors" are used to explain and discuss important developments, not only to the business community but also to other stakeholders and opinion formers. The communication strategy is regularly revisited and reinforced. The 2009 Communication Strategy and Public Relations Plan includes activities in the local, regional and national press alongside specific communication sector specific communication using editorials, a monthly digital newsletter on Better Regulation and portals to access information, as well as business ambassadors.[6]

ACTAL (*Adviescollege Toetsing Administratieve Lasten* – Advisory Board on Administrative Burdens) is a particularly important general ambassador and communicator for the government of its Better Regulation strategy. Not only is this part of its role, but it is engaged across the main Better Regulation policy "fronts" (burden reductions for business and citizens, EU level work, development of new regulations and impact assessment).

Ex post evaluation of Better Regulation

Evaluation processes have been embedded in or are being developed for some of the specific programmes that make up Better Regulation in the Netherlands. Notably, the programme on administrative burden reduction for businesses has been the subject of regular audits commissioned by the RRG, including from the World Bank and the OECD. The RRG notes that it intends to perform or commission regular evaluations of specific aspects such as the communications strategy, and progress in tackling larger administrative burdens. Progress on local Better Regulation initiatives (reduction of burdens, simplification of model regulations) has also been evaluated. For example, the effect of the work on model regulations for reducing administrative burdens has been evaluated by an external consultant. Evaluation of communication activities overall is part of the RRG communication strategy using a "perception monitor". The different activities are also evaluated separately. For instance the commercial campaign is evaluated by a specialised research company. There have also been some *ad hoc* evaluations of specific topics, for example the evaluation by ACTAL of awareness and capacities within government for tackling administrative burdens. There has not been any formal evaluation of the policies on law quality and on impact assessment for the development of new regulations.

The Netherlands Court of Audit (NCA) steps in with relevant audits on an *ad hoc* basis. It has evaluated the business burdens reduction programme twice, in 2006 and again in 2008 (when it also looked at the citizen programme). The NCA, which checks whether government policies represent "value for money" and which decides for itself what it should audit, chose to review this programme because of its cost, the political attention that it attracted, and its ambitious reach. It may carry out a further audit of the programme and its progress in achieving the latest 25% target. It has not yet carried out any evaluation of impact assessment, because it is a less obviously developed programme and not (as yet) very resource intensive.

The RRG has noted that evaluation of Better Regulation policy needs more investment. The aim is to take this forward with the introduction of "*het integrale afwegingskader beleid en wetgeving*" (integrated assessment framework for policy and legislation). This framework integrates the multitude of checks, guidelines and evaluations that have been developed over time with respect to specific elements of policy and legislation. The goal is to simplify the application of these checks, as well as promote their use, thus reinforcing their impact. The aim is to let this approach evolve gradually so that it becomes a comprehensive structural framework for evaluation.

E-Government in support of Better Regulation

The Netherlands have been formulating policies and programmes on e-Government since the mid-1990s, which makes them one of the early leaders in this field. E-Government is seen as a key lever of change in the bureaucracy and for Better Regulation.

The first step, the "National Action Plan on Electronic Highways" was set up in 1994. This was followed by a comprehensive programme in 1998 (focusing on provision of electronic access to government, quality of services to citizens and businesses, efficiency of service delivery though ICT usage). A dedicated unit was established in the Ministry of Interior and Kingdom Relations in 2001. The new cabinet in 2002 launched a new action plan, the so-called B4 (*Beter Beleid voor Burger en Bedrijf* – Better Government for Citizens and Businesses). The focus broadened from front-office activities to back-office infrastructure and the need for horizontal and vertical co-operation. In 2005 "Better Performance with ICT" was launched, with seven priorities: once-only data provision; electronic ID; faster on the Internet; trust and security; standardisation; consumer policy and ICT. An important development in 2006 was a strategic declaration which brought together the Ministry of Interior and the other levels of government – local authorities (VNG) the regions (IPO) and the water boards under the headline "Better Service, Less Administrative Burdens with Electronic Government". In 2007, the reference architecture "NORA 2.0" was published to underpin the aim of achieving a 65% target for the processing of public services in the provinces and municipalities.

The Ministry of Interior is responsible for overall co-ordination. Together with the Ministry of Economic Affairs, it shares responsibility for e-Government. The state secretaries of both ministries meet regularly to discuss common issues. Meetings also take place between civil servants on an *ad hoc* basis. The Interior State Secretary chairs a working group in which municipalities, provinces, and other relevant bodies are represented.

Reduction of administrative burdens has been described as the most important and tangible driver for the programme, and conversely, an essential component for the success of both the business and citizen burden reduction programmes. The XBRL project is one of several interesting and useful developments (Box 1.2).

Box 1.2. The Dutch XBRL Taxonomy Project

The standard electronic communication language XBRL is used for business and financial data (preparation, analysis and communication). It allows companies to prepare their data just once, but for it to be used several times over (data re use). The reporting company determines the scope of data to be prepared and transmitted on a case by case basis. XBRL provides the means to present the data to be prepared and transmitted in a structured manner and for processing to be automated. The advantages for "consumers" of financial data (investors, analysts, financial institutions, regulators) lies in the fact that it yields just one format of data, which aids evaluation, and reduces costs.

The first version of the XBRL taxonomy and technical infrastructure was available for reporting by business in the financial year 2006. After a hesitant start, business use of the system took off. Since January 2007, businesses and intermediaries can report their financial data using XBRL to various government entities (Chamber of Commerce, Tax Department, Statistics Netherlands).

An interesting development is applications in a broader context, for example credit reporting for the banks, and the development of simplified tax returns by tax consultants. The project can be seen as a laboratory for ideas to reduce further the burdens on businesses, and help to meet the 25% reduction target.

Another important development is a central portal for businesses, citizens and the public administration itself to access information and services (including regulations, licences, and public statements on regulatory and public service developments).[7] A search engine allows the user to browse the site, which also includes an "e-counter" (*Overheidsloket*), a one-stop shop for some interactive and transactional services.

However, it was also pointed out to the OECD review team that the use of ICT does not automatically support simplification – its value needs to be assessed on a case-by-case basis. The framework for the development of e-Government was generally considered to be an effective one. However, other comments to the team suggested that there was a need for more central management to frame a large number of projects (perhaps too many?), and the need to show results, given the resource intensiveness of many projects. The development of e-Government is acknowledged by the Dutch government to be a "work in progress" (as it is in all countries). Although the government has been active in the field for many years, coherence and complexity may be issues, and the extent to which projects and policies are effectively implemented on the ground, especially at local level. Recent conclusions of a commission (*Commissie Postma/Wallage*) were that infrastructure needs attention; there is a lack of consistency between ministries, and between the national and local levels. Proposals included making at least part of the infrastructure compulsory, to increase financial resources, and to monitor projects. Some of these conclusions echo the findings of the 2007 OECD report on e-Government (for example the need for more systematic monitoring and evaluation). Most of the commission's recommendations have been adopted by the government (OECD, 2007).

Most recently, a focus on projects has been put into a common e-Government programme, led by the Ministry of Interior. All levels of government (central government, provinces, local authorities and water boards) have committed themselves to have implemented a specific package of e-Government building blocks and services by 2011.

Notes

1. The 2007 World Bank report also raised the issue: "It is important that continued efforts to reduce administrative burdens are put in a context of other and often more significant regulatory impacts and risks".
2. This also provides external reviewers with valuable supporting evidence in their work.
3. For more, see the 1999 and 2007 OECD reports.
4. *Andere Overheid* – A different government.
5. *www.rr.nl.*
6. *www.rr.nl* and *www.antwoordvoorbedrijven.nl.*
7. *Overheid.nl.*

Chapter 2

Institutional capacities for Better Regulation

Regulatory management needs to find its place in a country's institutional architecture, and have support from all the relevant institutions. The institutional framework within which Better Regulation must exert influence extends well beyond the executive centre of government, although this is the main starting point. The legislature and the judiciary, regulatory agencies and the subnational levels of government, as well as international structures (notably, for this project, the EU), also play critical roles in the development, implementation and enforcement of policies and regulations.

The parliament may initiate new primary legislation, and proposals from the executive rarely if ever become law without integrating the changes generated by parliamentary scrutiny. The judiciary may have the role of constitutional guardian, and is generally responsible for ensuring that the executive acts within its proper authority, as well as playing an important role in the interpretation and enforcement of regulations. Regulatory agencies and subnational levels of government may exercise a range of regulatory responsibilities. They may be responsible (variously) for the development of secondary regulations, issue guidance on regulations, have discretionary powers to interpret regulations, enforce regulations, as well as influencing the development of the overall policy and regulatory framework. What role should each actor have, taking into account accountability, feasibility, and balance across government? What is the best way to secure effective institutional oversight of Better Regulation policies?

The OECD's previous country reviews highlight the fact that the institutional context for implanting effective regulatory management is complex and often highly fragmented. Approaches need to be customised, as countries' institutional settings and legal systems can be very specific, ranging from systems adapted to small societies with closely knit governments that rely on trust and informality, to large federal systems that must find ways of dealing with high levels of autonomy and diversity.

Continuous training and capacity building within government, supported by adequate financial resources, contributes to the effective application of Better Regulation. Beyond the technical need for training in certain processes such as impact assessment or plain drafting, training communicates the message to administrators that this is an important issue, recognised as such by the administrative and political hierarchy. It can be seen as a measure of the political commitment to Better Regulation. It also fosters a sense of ownership for reform initiatives, and enhances co-ordination and regulatory coherence.

Assessment and recommendations

The establishment of the Regulatory Reform Group (RRG) has been a major step forward in providing a clearer focus for Better Regulation. The merger of several relevant units out of two core and influential ministries – finance and economic affairs – responsible for the business-related part of Better Regulation policy into the RRG was the right move. The RRG has established itself as a well known and vigorous Better Regulation entity not only with the business community within the Netherlands, but also across Europe and with the EU institutions. The merger also signals that Better Regulation policy in the Netherlands has reached a certain level of sustainability across coalition and cabinet political cycles, since the RRG is a continuation and strengthening of units set up under previous governments.

The RRG, however, only covers business aspects of the government's Better Regulation policy. Two other key ministries for Better Regulation are not part of the RRG structure. The Ministry of Justice has long played a critical role in managing the development of new regulations and is currently seeking to develop a new and stronger approach to impact assessment. The Ministry of Interior and Kingdom Relations is not only responsible for reducing burdens on citizens, professionals and inter-governmental aspects, but also has general co-ordinating responsibility for key issues related to Better Regulation – e-Government, general co-ordination of the municipalities and the enforcement inspectorates, and for the civil service (including civil service reform), as well as general relations with the parliament. The Ministry of Foreign Affairs is responsible for important aspects of the general management of EU regulations.

In this context, the establishment of the Steering Group for Better Regulation was a positive move to strengthen links between the key Better Regulation ministries. The Steering Group for Better Regulation, chaired by the Prime Minister, meets every quarter and brings together the Ministry of Interior, Ministry of Justice, Ministry of Finance and Ministry of Economic Affairs. It is supported by an officials group. It reviews progress reports on Better Regulation policies and prepares the ground for cabinet and parliamentary reports. The OECD peer review team were told that, from low key beginnings, this group had started to become more proactive, in response to the more controversial phase of reform that the Netherlands now appears to be entering.

The independent watchdog ACTAL is another important institutional asset helping to hold different parts of the agenda together. Since it was established in 2000, ACTAL has played an important role in helping to motivate and structure regulatory reform in the Netherlands (and provided inspiration for other countries to set up similar structures, most recently in Sweden). It is not only important for its challenge function to government. It also, alongside the Steering Group on Better Regulation, covers several elements of Better Regulation (the business and citizen burden reduction programmes, advice to the cabinet on the burdens of new regulations which gives it a role in *ex ante* impact assessment, and promotion of Better Regulation at EU level).

An effective institutional framework has also been established for sharing the Better Regulation agenda with the local levels of government. Municipalities have a key interface with business and citizens via their enforcement, planning and licensing responsibilities. The central government agreement with the municipalities and its linked Better Regulation action plan provides shape and substance to the roll out of shared Better Regulation goals, such as meeting burden reduction targets.

The central institutional framework for overseeing Better Regulation in its entirety remains, however, relatively weak and fragmented. The Steering Group for Better

Regulation, which unites the four main ministries, has so far played an uncertain contribution to the Better Regulation agenda. It does not, for example, appear to have yet played a defining role in promoting the development of a new impact assessment process, which needs a strong central lead to encourage cross ministerial co-operation. This relative fragmentation stands in the way of an even stronger Better Regulation performance. It also means that responsibilities – who does what – are not clear to stakeholders outside the system, and that the system itself does not provide an optimal framework for tackling next steps, notably the development of a stronger impact assessment process, and perhaps also a stronger and mutually supportive relationship between the business and citizen burden reduction programmes. The Ministry of Foreign Affairs is not part of the group, which is at odds with the fact that it plays an important role in the management of EU regulations, and these account for a high share of the total.

What should be done to strengthen the institutional oversight framework? The radical option would be to expand the RRG's role and structure so that it includes relevant units from other ministries engaged in Better Regulation (Interior, Justice, and also perhaps – building on the existing interaction between the RRG and a Better Regulation co-ordinator at the Ministry of Foreign Affairs – a stronger link with that ministry). However this may not be the most effective way to strengthen co-operation between ministries which each have a strong and distinctive contribution to bring. Short of this option, it is essential that the Steering Group on Better Regulation and its supporting group of officials start to play a more proactive role, based on a well-defined agenda that includes the development of the impact assessment process. In that case, the RRG, as the current main focal point for Better Regulation in the Netherlands, would appear to be best placed to provide the secretariat for the group, perhaps including secondments from other ministries. Strong institutional links between the Ministry of Justice and the other ministries are especially important. The Ministry of Justice is a key player through its role in overseeing legal quality. The OECD's report ten years ago picked up the issue, and the World Bank picked it up again in 2007 (Box 2.1).

Box 2.1. Recommendation and comments from the 1999 OECD report: Institutional issues

Better co-ordinate regulatory reform and regulatory quality initiatives

There are opportunities to improve the degree of co-ordination between the various regulatory quality assurance and regulatory reform initiatives being undertaken in the Netherlands. Improved co-ordination would be particularly beneficial between RIA and consultation processes, between the Ministry of Justice' legislative quality assurance work (including the Directives on Legislation and the scrutiny of Bills process) and RIA and between RIA and programmes aimed at using regulatory alternatives.

There does not seem to be a clear relationship, or co-ordination, between the Directives on legislation, and the Ministry of Justice assessment of legislative quality, on the one hand, and the RIA process and role of the Ministry of Economic Affairs on the other. This appears to reflect the historically dominant role of the Ministry of Justice in regard to legislative policy and a consequent tendency to view legislative quality as primarily a technical legal concept, rather than as one which has a distinct, and possibly paramount, economics/public policy aspect.

Addressing this issue appears to require a role for the Ministry of Economic Affairs that is more integrated with the Ministry of Justice' work on legislative quality assessment. In addition, formulation of legislative quality guidelines covering economic and public policy aspects of quality that are distinct from (though co-ordinated with) a more streamlined set of "legal" guidelines should be considered. Here again there is a need for a strong co-operative relationship between the two ministries. Moreover, the latter guidelines should be presented in the context of a strengthened set of RIA requirements.

Comments from the 2007 World Bank report

At the core of this should be consideration of lead responsibility for impact assessment with the burden reduction programme. Individual ministries would remain responsible for their own projects and for preparing impact assessments.

Recommendation 2.1. The government should consider the best way in which the institutional oversight framework for Better Regulation can be strengthened. The Steering Group on Better Regulation and its supporting group of officials should in any event play a more proactive role, based on a well-defined agenda that includes the development of the impact assessment process.

The need for further support for, and culture change among, implementing ministries needs to be addressed. This is not a new issue (the OECD's 1999 report had already noted it – see Box 2.2), and not unique to the Netherlands. It was raised by several stakeholders with the OECD peer review team. ACTAL, for example, drew attention to the evidence of its attitude surveys and said that a measure of success might be when it could be disbanded (not yet). The increasing complexity of the modern reform agenda is a factor. Ministries face a number of challenges for which they need to be well prepared. Stakeholders are more demanding (sometimes both requesting more freedom as well as criticising regulatory failures). The Better Regulation agenda has been broadened to cover the different levels of government. The burden reduction programmes are starting to address more controversial issues. Civil service reforms add a further layer of complexity as well as opportunity (resources are being cut, but at the same time this means that old habits can be rethought, as demonstrated by the inspections reform programme). As well as the need for support through enhanced guidance and training, effective carrots and sticks for change need to be in place. The strong link that has been established between showing results for the business burden reduction programme and the budget cycle is helpful. The RRG training and guidance on Better Regulation tools is also important.

Box 2.2. Recommendation and comments from the 1999 OECD report: Culture change

Strengthen accountability for results within the ministries through development of measurable and public performance standards for regulatory reform.

Capacities for central direction are not balanced by effective incentives for the ministries to change themselves, particularly given offsetting pressures from their constituencies and from the political level. In particular, the objectives of the regulatory reform programme are formulated at a high-level of generality, and transparent measures of performance for each Ministry have not been adopted. That is, objectives are strategic rather than results-oriented. Hence, accountability for results is over-centralised, whereas the skills and resources for reform are decentralised. The fact that incentives for the ministries to produce good regulation are still not very strong may be one explanation for why the regulatory habits of the administration have not changed very much.

If the scope, depth, and pace of reform is to increase, the programme should mobilise the energies of the line ministries by reforming incentive structures through development of performance standards for quality regulation, and linkage of those standards to fiscal budgeting and other credible review mechanisms.

Recommendation 2.2. The government should review whether incentives for culture change could be strengthened. For example it should review whether the link to the budget cycle for setting targets and assessing performance needs to be given sharper teeth (real consequences for ministerial budgets, effect on the performance appraisal of key officials). Further support for ministries in the shape of guidance and training should also be put in place.

The parliament plays a particularly important role in the development of the Better Regulation agenda in the Netherlands. A key player beyond the executive is the parliament. The Dutch political system works on the basis of coalition agreements which set the policy framework for the four years of the electoral cycle. The parliament holds the government closely accountable for implementation of the coalition agreements.[1] It is regularly sent progress reports on different aspects of the Better Regulation programme, and has itself initiated reform of inspections policy. With the extension of the Better Regulation agenda into more difficult and complex territory, its support will be critical.

Recommendation 2.3. The government should take active steps to develop a dialogue with relevant parliamentary committees in order to encourage a shared vision of Better Regulation goals and their contribution to wider public policy goals (see also recommendation in Chapter 5 on the business burden reduction programme).

Background

General institutional context

Developments in the general institutional context

The main development has been at the local level. The Dualisation of Municipal Government Act 2002 separated the powers of municipal councils and executives – municipal executive members can no longer be members of the municipal councils. This was followed by the Dualisation of Provincial Government Act 2003 which did the same for provincial councils and executives. The executives are the administrators, while the councils set the agenda, scrutinise the administration, and represent the citizens. There is a slow but growing perception that the changes have resulted in greater council independence, as well as some concerns that bureaucracy has also increased.

The number of municipalities has steadily fallen over time – from 1 064 in 1936 to 443 today – as part of the central government's policy to improve administrative quality and effectiveness through mergers. The size of population per municipality has also grown in consequence, also because of population growth.[2]

There are ongoing changes in the civil service from the reform programme aimed at making it more efficient. This has encouraged some streamlining, for example in the inspectorates responsible for enforcement.

Box 2.3. Institutional framework for the Netherlands policy, law making and law execution process

The Kingdom of the Netherlands is a parliamentary constitutional monarchy.

The executive

There are thirteen ministries, each headed by a minister (sometimes two), supported by one of more state secretaries. Ministers cannot at the same time be members of the parliament. The civil service is politically neutral. Each ministry is headed by a civil servant secretary general. Policy must be adopted collectively. Policy making is based on a network of ministerial committees, ultimately reporting to the cabinet, which meets weekly. Policy and legislative proposals go to the relevant ministerial committees, after discussions at official level.

The legislature

The Dutch parliament has two chambers. The House of Representatives is responsible for enacting all new legislation and for approving amendments to existing legislation. The Senate also scrutinises legislation but can only accept or reject draft legislation in its entirety. The legislative process can be protracted, and it can take five or six years for a bill to become law. Bills are often amended in their passage through the parliament. There is a structure of standing, general and theme committees. Elections are based on a system of proportional representation, under which each party is allocated a number of seats in the parliament corresponding to the proportion of the overall vote won by that party. Because of the large number of political parties resulting from this system, the country is always governed by coalitions. There is currently a coalition majority in the parliament.

Coalition agreements

Each government works on the basis of coalition agreements (*coalitieakkoord*) which set the policy framework for the four years of the electoral cycle, and annual budget plans. Together these generate proposals for policy/legislation.

The judiciary

The Dutch judicial system is based on the traditions of continental Europe, with a codified law and a written Constitution. The Council of State is a form of constitutional court, advising the government on all draft bills and orders in council.

The court system consists of courts, courts of appeal, and a Supreme Court. Administrative appeals are heard by the administrative branch of the courts. The judiciary can and does interpret the law in its rulings, but cannot challenge it.

Regulatory agencies

There are broadly three types of regulatory agency, generally linked to a parent ministry: enforcement inspectorates; autonomous administrative bodies whose tasks generally require the strict and independent application of regulations in individual cases; and agencies for industry and the professions, with statutory powers over their members, the employer/employee Social and Economic Council being the most important.

Local levels of government

The Netherlands is a decentralised unitary state with three tiers of government. It is divided into twelve provinces and 443 municipalities. Each province and municipality has its own council, elected by popular vote. Their executives are chaired by provincial governors (Queen's commissioners) and mayors, who are appointed by the central government, and who also chair their council.

Provincial and municipal authorities have important implementation and enforcement (including inspection) functions, especially in physical and environmental planning, and in licensing, based on regulations laid down by central government. They have limited powers to make their own regulations (by-laws) on matters that directly affect them, but they may also make additional regulations within the framework of national regulations.

Developments in Better Regulation institutions

The first main institutional home for what started out as deregulation policy in the 1980s was the Ministry of Justice, responsible (as it remains today) for legal quality, defined to include early forms of impact assessment on new regulations. With the launch of the *MDW* programme in 1994, which broadened the regulatory policy agenda by linking it to market liberalisation as well as legal quality, responsibility became shared with the Ministry of Economic Affairs. At this stage, small units in each ministry co-ordinated and managed the relevant projects.

The institutional focus broadened further from 2001, with the development of policies aimed at reducing administrative burdens, first for business and then for citizens, which drew in the Ministry of Finance and Ministry of Interior. An inter-ministerial unit for administrative burdens on business (IPAL), originally based in the Ministry of Economic Affairs, was moved after the 2003 election to the Ministry of Finance in May 2003. In 2007, IPAL merged with other relevant units in the Ministry of Economic Affairs to become today's Regulatory Reform Group (RRG). A separate project team *Projectdirectie Administratieve Lasten* (PAL) was established in 2003 in the Ministry of Interior to cover burdens on citizens. In 2007 PAL became REAL (Programme Bureaucratic Simplification) and now covers administrative burdens for citizens, professionals in the public sector and intergovernmental burdens. Also noteworthy is the establishment of ACTAL, the independent watchdog, in 2000.

Table 2.1. Milestones in the development of Better Regulation institutions in the Netherlands

1984-89	Ministry of Justice and Prime Minister's Office are the main focus of Better Regulation activity (expansion of Directives on Legislation related to law drafting quality issues beyond technical matters). Council of State is also involved in advising on first steps in reinforcing the quality framework.
1989-94	Ministry of Justice is given explicit responsibility for legislative policy and the General Legislative Policy Division is created. It issues legislative policies guidance paper "Legislation in Perspective" with cabinet authority, and further revises the Directives on Legislation.
1994	The *MDW* programme which broadens the regulatory policy agenda leads to a sharing of responsibility between the Ministry of Justice and the Ministry of Economic Affairs. Small units in each ministry co-ordinate and manage projects.
1995	The *Werkgroep voorgenomen regelgeving* (Working Group on proposed legislation) is established, a joint committee of the ministries of Economic Affairs, Environment and Justice.
2000	ACTAL is established as the independent review body for the programme on administrative simplification, to work on the basis of the recommendations of the *Slechte* Committee.
2003	IPAL is founded. The Inter-ministerial Unit for Administrative Burdens (IPAL).was set up in May 2003 to manage the programme for reducing administrative burdens on business, was originally located in the Ministry of Economic Affairs, but was moved to the Ministry of Finance after the 2003 election. The Working Group on proposed legislation is renamed to *Gezamenlijk steunpunt voorgenomen regelgeving and Meldpunt voorgenomen regelgeving* (Proposed legislation desk).
2005	Ministerial Steering Group for Better Regulation – chaired by the Prime Minister – is formed, meeting on an *ad hoc* basis.
2007	The Regulatory Reform Group – a merger between IPAL of the Ministry of Finance and some units of the Ministry of Economic Affairs – is created. PAL becomes Programme for Bureaucratic Simplification (REAL) and includes reduction of administrative burdens of professionals in the public sector and intergovernmental burdens. Formal establishment of the Ministerial Steering Group for Better Regulation, chaired by the Prime Minister.
2007	The Inspection Council is established in order to stimulate a structural and intensive co-operation between the inspectorates of the different ministries. A main goal of this co-operation is the reduction of unnecessary burdens caused by multiple inspections ACTAL's term of office is prolonged until 2011

Source: Dutch government

Key institutional players for Better Regulation policy

The executive centre of government

Key ministries

The ministries of Finance, Economic Affairs, Justice and the Interior share responsibility for Better Regulation policy, each from a different angle. The Ministry of Finance and the Ministry of Economic Affairs share responsibility for co-ordinating and monitoring the business programme for regulatory burden reduction, for which they have established a shared directorate, the Regulatory Reform Group. The Ministry of Justice is responsible for legal quality, defined broadly. The Ministry of Interior and Kingdom Relations is responsible for a range of relevant cross-cutting issues including e-Government, the citizens' programme for administrative burden reduction, general co-ordination of the municipalities (including their financial oversight) and the inspectorates, for the civil service (including civil service reforms), and general relations with the parliament.[3]

The Regulatory Reform Group

The Regulatory Reform Group (*Regiegroep Regeldruk* – RRG) was established in 2007 as a successor to the Inter-ministerial Unit for Administrative Burdens (IPAL). IPAL, set up in May 2003 to manage the programme for reducing administrative burdens on business, was originally located in the Ministry of Economic Affairs, but was moved to the Ministry of Finance after the 2003 election. This move was intended to strengthen the unit's position within government and not least, to create a stronger link to the budget cycle. IPAL continued to co-operate closely with the Ministry of Economic Affairs, and in 2007 it was decided to merge IPAL and three project groups in the Ministry of Economic Affairs (responsible among other issues for the business impact assessment) into a single entity that reports simultaneously to both ministries.

The Regulatory Reform Group is jointly "owned" (staffed and financed) by the Ministry of Finance and the Ministry of Economic Affairs, and reports to their state secretaries (junior ministers). It is physically located in the Ministry. It has a staff of 40,[4] half of whom originate from the two ministries (Finance and Economic Affairs).The RRG is divided into teams formed around ten themes, varying in size. The themes are: measuring targets; planning and control (monitoring); ICT; international co-operation (including the EU); municipalities; interaction with the business community; advising the Council of Ministers; communication; quality of service delivery; and overall management. Most staff members belong to several teams.

The RRG covers the following main activities:

- *Day-to-day co-ordination and monitoring of the business burdens reduction programme.* The RRG has "account managers" for each ministry who interact daily with counterparts in ministries (which each have a satellite contact). They monitor the development of specific reduction measures for each ministry on proposed new legislation which is submitted to cabinet. If this is expected to generate administrative burdens, they try to intervene as quickly as possible. Account managers visit their ministries at least four times a year to review progress and results. When specific draft legislation is under development contact will be considerably more frequent.

- *Monitoring, advice and reporting at the political level.* The state secretaries for the two ministries have regular discussions with each minister, to review progress toward meeting the reduction target, opportunities and challenges for progress. Reports are then submitted to the cabinet, so that it can discuss overall progress. Full reports to the parliament are made twice a year and there are two abridged reports as well, making four reports in total each year.[5] The reporting structure to the parliament is linked to the reporting cycle of the budget (with key documents to the parliament in September and May). This means that the round of budget negotiations with respective ministers is preceded by a round of bilateral talks about the progress on their respective regulatory burden reduction programmes, allowing this – if necessary – to be discussed further in the budget talks.

- *Co-ordination of EU policy regarding administrative burden reduction for business.* This includes bilateral contacts with other member states and the European Commission. Since 2007 the RRG has invested heavily in the Dutch inter-ministerial framework for addressing substantial regulatory burdens for businesses arising from EU regulations. This is reflected in the revised 2008 Dutch guidelines for the preparation of the national position on new EU proposals. The RRG interacts regularly with the Ministry of Foreign Affairs co-ordinator for EU matters.

- *Development of methodology, education and training of civil servants.* This includes risk analysis of burden reduction initiatives, and *ex post* measurements of the efficiency of burden reduction initiatives. The RRG has provided training for ministries in the use of the Standard Cost Methodology (SCM). Workshops have also been organised, together with ACTAL and REAL. A standard module "regulatory impact" has been established and is currently being developed for inclusion in the general introductory training courses for civil servants.

Programme Regulatory and Administrative Burdens

Programme Regulatory and Administrative Burdens (*Regeldruk en Administratieve Lasten* - REAL) was established in 2007 as a successor to the Programme Administrative Burden Reduction (PAL). PAL was set up in 2003 to manage the programme for reducing administrative burdens on citizens. The programme is located in the Ministry of the Interior and Kingdom Relations.

REAL has a staff of 18 and co-ordinates three different projects: reduction of (administrative) burdens for citizens, reduction of administrative burdens for professionals in the public sector, and the reduction of intergovernmental administrative burdens. A common approach is being used in all three projects, which includes a focus on bottlenecks and the use of typical profiles.

REAL's activities cover similar ground to that of the RRG:

- *Day to day co-ordination and monitoring of the three burden reduction programmes.* The difference is that REAL does not have account managers for each ministry, but it does monitor proposed new legislation which is submitted to Cabinet.

- *Monitoring, advice and reporting at the political level.* REAL monitors progress towards meeting the reduction target in a similar way to the RRG. An annual report on progress is submitted to the cabinet and to the parliament.

- *Addressing administrative burdens of citizens at the EU level and exchange of knowledge and experience with other European countries.* This is not as extensively developed as the approach of the RRG, especially concerning the EU level. However, several actions have been taken to address administrative burdens for citizens at the EU level and an informal network on administrative burdens for citizens has been established.

- *Development of methodology, education and training of civil servants.* REAL is, specifically, a pioneer in studies concerning the qualitative side of administrative burdens and improvements in the quality of service delivery, via the identification of the most important irritations and bottlenecks, using the concept of trust as a vehicle to reduce burdens, and the development of profiles and role models. In addition REAL facilitates several courses for officials in areas such as mediation techniques and the development of simpler forms.

Co-ordination across central government

Prime Minister's Office and the Ministerial Steering Group for Better Regulation

There is a relatively small Prime Minister's Office (PMO).[6] The PMO co-ordinates work across government on the six pillars of the coalition agreement which give high-level shape to government policy over the electoral cycle. The PMO also chairs a Ministerial Steering Group for Better Regulation, which meets every quarter. This group is supported by an officials' group drawn from the four key Better Regulation ministries (Interior, Justice, Finance, and Economic Affairs). The Steering Group started informally during the last cabinet term and has now taken more formal shape. The group monitors progress on the different aspects of the Better Regulation policy, including the programmes for the reduction of administrative burdens on business and on citizens, and the Ministry of Justice's programme to improve law making.

Regulatory agencies

The fourteen national enforcement inspectorates are playing an important role, alongside the municipalities, in the current reform of enforcement policy toward a more risk-based approach. The practical roll-out of the reform programme is overseen by the Inspection Council.

The legislature

The parliament holds the government closely accountable for implementation of the coalition agreements that underpin the electoral cycle. For example, the cabinet reported annually to the parliament on progress with the 2003-07 programme for public sector reform (*Andere Overheid – A Different Government*). Although there is no specific committee for Better Regulation, the parliament takes a keen interest in reports on progress, and has started several initiatives for reform. The RRG reports, through cabinet, four times a year to the parliament on progress with the policy to reduce administrative burdens for business, and the Ministry of Interior also reports regularly on its projects including the citizen programme. The parliament was instrumental in pushing for a new approach to inspections and enforcement. There are regular progress reports to the parliament on enforcement policy, including the Inspection Council's annual report. The European Affairs Committee plays an important role in the scrutiny of EU legislation.

The judiciary

No special issues or developments were drawn to the team's attention in the review.[7] The judiciary appears to play a relatively low-key role in Better Regulation issues.

Local levels of government

As in most other OECD countries with a unitary structure, municipalities have a key interface with business and citizens, via their enforcement, planning and licensing responsibilities. The provincial level is mainly relevant in this context for its role in environmental matters. There is a complex and close relationship between the local levels and the national level. Local government is independent of central government. At the same time the mayors are not elected locally, but are political appointments and so have close links with central government.

Other important players

Advisory Board on Administrative Burdens

ACTAL (*Adviescollege Toetsing Administratieve Lasten* – Advisory Board on Administrative Burdens) is an independent regulatory review body which was originally set up in 2000 for a period of three years. It has been renewed twice, and was recently given a further lease of life until 2011. It has a board of three, and a secretariat of twelve.[8] It was originally set up to advise the government on the impact of proposed new regulations on business, but its remit has been steadily expanded to encompass other Better Regulation policies as they emerged. Its current mission thus also covers the citizens' programme for the reduction of administrative burdens. For the remainder of its term ACTAL will pay special attention to culture change within ministries with regard to regulatory impacts. ACTAL's annual work programme is endorsed by the Minister of Finance and the Minister of Interior and Kingdom Relations, who then submit it to the parliament.

ACTAL's current tasks are to advise the government and the parliament on:

- Administrative burdens for businesses and citizens as a result of proposed regulation.
- Programmes and measures regarding the reduction of administrative burdens for businesses and citizens as a result of existing regulation.
- Strategic issues on the subject of regulatory burden, part of which is the advising on the development and the use of the integral assessment framework in preparing policy and regulation.

It also advises local and regional governments on regulatory burdens, upon their written request.

The Netherlands Court of Audit

The Netherlands Court of Audit (NCA) provides *ex post* scrutiny of government actions. It investigates whether public funds have been collected and spent legitimately, efficiently and effectively. It is independent of the government and the parliament. It decides for itself what to audit, how to do so and what to publish, although it considers requests from government and the parliament. That said it considers the parliament, to which it is ultimately accountable for its own management, to be its main "customer", and seeks to gear its work programme to meet the needs of the parliament. It publishes an annual programme of audit projects. Reports set out factual findings, and make recommendations for improvement. The NCA has carried out two audits of the programme for administrative burden reduction on business, and an audit of the transposition of EU directives. The government wants to reduce the cost of auditing (part of the proposed 25% cut in the civil service), and the NCA's response to this is that a stronger policy to address regulation inside government could release resources.

Resources and training

At the national level there are approximately 100 officials directly involved in Better Regulation, on a total of more than 100 000 (approximate figure) officials in the national public service.[9]

Training in Better Regulation is picked up in several ways. In 2000, the Ministry of Justice set up an Academy for Legislation, which provides "on the job" training for legal drafters, including Better Regulation. The policy academies set up by some other ministries for training in policy making also cover aspects of Better Regulation policy. The RRG provides training and support for ministry officials in the SCM methodology and burden reduction (see above). A positive recent development has been the establishment of training on regulatory management techniques, including *ex ante* impact assessment and regulatory burden management.

There is an important general link between Better Regulation and the roll out of the "Modernising Central Government Programme", which has the objective of a smaller and more effective central government.[10] Culture change has some way to go as regards Better Regulation. Studies were commissioned by ACTAL and conducted in early 2005 and late 2006 by the Institute for Research on Public Expenditure (IOO), to measure the attention given to administrative burdens in ministries. The research found that there has been only marginal change in the "internalisation" by ministries of knowledge, attitude and behaviour towards administrative burdens.[11] There is some way to go with culture change.

Notes

1. The fact that government ministers cannot at the same time be members of the parliament explains part of this.
2. An average of 33 744 people were resident in a municipality in 2006, almost triple the figure of 1960.
3. The ministry also mentioned "plain Dutch" in its interview with the OECD peer review team.
4. This compares with a smaller IPAL staff of the equivalent of 18 full-time positions, of which 7 were on secondment from line ministries.
5. There were two reports originally, but the parliament asked for more.
6. 497 staff, 0.4% of all national civil servants.

7. In some countries there can be issues – for example an increase in appeals, or delays in court judgements.

8. The board currently consists of Mr. Steven van Eijck, Mrs. Francine Giskes and Mr. Tjark de Lange, who between them have significant experience of public administration and politics, the business sector, and public administration related to administrative burdens for citizens.

9. Assuming EUR 100 000 per official the overall budget can be estimated at around EUR 10 million.

10. Twenty per cent reduction in staff over four years by 2011 (25% in policy departments, 5-16% in executive agencies, 5% in the tax office).

11. The reports are based on surveys of 670 and 1 460 civil servants and policy officials. Both studies achieved a high response: 79% in 2005 and 67% in 2006. These "internalisation studies" measured what civil servants know about administrative burdens (knowledge), what they think about them (attitude) and how they deal with them (behaviour). Internalisation is expressed as an unweighted average of the scores for knowledge, attitude and behaviour and amounted to 49% in 2005 and 53% in 2006. This means that the culture shift in the 18 months between the two studies improved by merely four percentage points.

Chapter 3

Transparency through consultation and communication

Transparency is one of the central pillars of effective regulation, supporting accountability, sustaining confidence in the legal environment, making regulations more secure and accessible, less influenced by special interests, and therefore more open to competition, trade and investment. It involves a range of actions including standardised procedures for making and changing regulations, consultation with stakeholders, effective communication and publication of regulations and plain language drafting, codification, controls on administrative discretion, and effective appeals processes. It can involve a mix of formal and informal processes. Techniques such as common commencement dates can make it easier for business to digest regulatory requirements. The contribution of e-Government to improve transparency, consultation and communication is of growing importance.

This chapter focuses on two main elements of transparency: public consultation and communication on regulations (other aspects are considered elsewhere in the text – for example appeals are considered in Chapter 6).[1]

Assessment and recommendations

Public consultation on regulations

There is a need for rapid improvement of public consultation as an integral part of effective regulatory management. The Netherlands appears to be at a cross-roads between longstanding traditions of very structured consultation (via the search for a consensus through established groups and committees, and the commissioning of expert advice), and the development of new approaches which reach out to stakeholders very differently, not least via the Internet. There is an increasingly urgent need to take stock and to improve and update the approach to consultation. This does not imply wholesale abandonment of the traditional approaches, but there is a need to boost transparency and ensure that effective and timely consultation is integral to the development of government policies and in particular to the impact assessment process for new regulations. The business and citizen burden reduction programmes have shown the way with new approaches to capture more effectively the real concerns of stakeholders. The pilot project for Internet-based consultation on new regulations across ministries looks very promising.

Recommendation 3.1. The plans to introduce Internet-based consultation should be pursued, with special attention to accessibility by the general public. Public consultation should be woven into the impact assessment process for new regulations. A code of good practice to be followed by ministries and others with significant responsibilities for new regulations might also be considered.

Public communication on regulations

The introduction of Common Commencement Dates (CCD) is a very positive step forward. This will put the Netherlands ahead of many other OECD countries. CCDs are fundamentally helpful to business. The presentation to the business community with a set of new regulations "in one shot" may need some management to ensure that it does not (perversely) contribute to poor perceptions of the government's control over the flow of new regulations.

Background

Public consultation on regulations

Traditional approaches to public consultation[2]

The traditional Dutch approach to consultation is based on the corporatist philosophy, resting on two principles, the search for consensus, and the search for expert advice to improve regulatory quality. There is a particularly strong attachment to consensus building in the development of new policies and regulations. The corporatist idea is to introduce checks and balances into the decision making, to increase the legitimacy of regulation, to identify "acceptable" policies and thereby increase the level of compliance. Another perceived advantage is that it ensures affected parties are well informed in advance of proposed new regulation, and can minimise adjustment costs through forward planning. The principles have given rise to two formal and distinct consultation structures:

- *A wide range of formal advisory bodies*, to provide the advisory function. These bodies have been created *ad hoc* by individual legislation to work closely with ministries on policy issues of strategic importance. They are explicitly recognised as "permanent advisory bodies for matters of legislation and administration of the state" by the Constitution. The most important is the Council of State. [3]

- *A separate network of advisory bodies,* created under the Industrial Organisation Act 1950, to represent the consultation function. The tripartite principle is the underlying factor determining representation. The main body is the Social and Economic Council (SER), made up of 15 members representing employers, 15 for employees, and 15 independent experts appointed by the government. These bodies also have significant regulatory power covering their members in areas such as registration, wages, and training.

The system, however, came under considerable criticism in the 1990s, as unsuited to modern realities. The Dutch government responded with a range of reforms, notably a drastic reduction in the number of advisory boards, and removal of the legal requirement for the government to consult advisory bodies (Law on Advisory Bodies of 1996). Alongside these reforms, ministries started turning to other, more flexible and open consultation approaches, on their own initiative, including notice and comment.

Box 3.1. Comments from the 1999 OECD report: Consultation

The report noted the following criticisms levied at the system:

- They have severely dampened policy responsiveness. On average, seven years was required to introduce new legislation, a considerable fraction of which was traditionally spent in consultation.
- The separation of "advice and consultation" has been compromised in practice. Advisory bodies have too often functioned as defenders of narrow self-interests, rather than as providers of expertise.
- As the *Commissie Geelhoed* found, extensive consultation based on the search for consensus promotes regulatory complexity, as additional details are added in an attempt to balance competing interests.
- By "locking in" consensus solutions at an early stage, the advisory and tripartite bodies have been accused of limiting the role and freedom to act of the government and the parliament.
- The corporatist and cartel-like structures established under the Industrial Organisation Act are increasingly inconsistent with EU single market policies, particularly competition principles.
- Changes in Dutch society, including a decline in union membership and the rise in other forms of social organisation, meant that the representativeness and hence the legitimacy of the tripartite structures was diminished. The Dutch government stated in 1993 that *"The desired social base cannot always be obtained by consulting advisory bodies"*.[4]

The Dutch government (has) responded with significant reforms:

The number of advisory boards was drastically reduced, from 491 in 1976 to 161 in 1991 and 108 in 1993. A yet more radical reform in 1997 abolished all 108 remaining bodies and replaced them with a single advisory body for each Ministry. This reform aims to clearly separate advice and consultation, and to refocus these bodies to major policy issues away from details. The oversight ministries are concerned that too many consultative groups have been re-established following the abolition, but they believe that the change has, nonetheless, improved the situation. Old habits die hard, however, and, without limits on their numbers, there is a continuing danger of proliferation of "new" advisory bodies.

Another fundamental change taken in 1997 is removal of the legal requirement for the government to consult advisory bodies. This follows a more limited change implemented in 1994 (via the General Administrative Law Act) abolishing the consultative requirement in cases where legislation is limited to implementing binding EU legislation. Both of these changes affect the peak consultative bodies (the SER and Council of State). A time limit of three months was also imposed for the provision of advice to reduce the contribution of consultation to the length of the Dutch legislation-making process.

The OECD report also noted that, alongside these reforms, ministries started turning to other, more flexible and open consultation approaches, on their own initiative. It noted evidence of the increasing use of informal consultation to do the real work of consensus-building, with traditional methods becoming more of a formality to confirm the outcome. Notice and comment[5] had also started to be used, albeit infrequently.

The OECD report concluded:

"Together, these reforms represent a major overhaul of virtually all aspects of consultation. By giving the administration greater flexibility on who to consult and when, these reforms have sought to enhance the value-added of consultation in producing hard data and expert opinion, and to streamline the process and reduce delays. Increased use of open "notice and comment" processes aims to increase participation by a greater range of interests. The reforms are consistent with an international trend toward more transparent and accessible regulatory processes.

Recent developments

The traditional approaches have increasingly been paralleled by novel forms of consultation arising from the deployment of some Better Regulation policies, notably the policies to reduce administrative burdens on business and on citizens. This has "opened" up the system to new methods and engaged relevant stakeholders more directly and *ad hoc* than before:

- The business regulatory burden reduction programme has deployed a range of approaches to solicit the views of the business community, including an interactive website[6] and the "adoption" by ministers of companies in order to meet them regularly for a better understanding of their concerns.

- The citizen programme has also deployed a range of processes to capture citizen concerns, including seminars and workshops, and citizens panels.

By contrast, consultation on other Better Regulation policies and for the development of specific regulations has not evolved as strongly. Consultation is not an issue that is covered formally in the current impact assessment process for the development of new regulations.

A general recent initiative by the Ministry of Justice is a two-year experiment with Internet consultation on new regulations across all ministries, due to start in summer 2009. An evaluation report on which the government will make a decision for full introduction will be sent to the parliament in 2010. The experiment draws from the experiences of other countries (United Kingdom, European Union). Each ministry will select at least 10 % of new regulations to be covered by the new approach, one of the criteria being the impact of the regulation on administrative burdens. Ministers must post a specific proposal (with specific information about expected effects, and questions to be answered) on the Internet for at least four weeks (maximum 12 weeks), on which anyone is invited to give a reaction. A consolidated feedback report on the results must be posted on the Internet at the end of the process, and the outcome of the consultation is expected to be reflected in the draft regulation. Some ministries (Justice, Finance) have already carried out Internet consultations on new regulations such as the regulations on simplifying company law and the law on financial governance.

Public communication on regulations

Accessibility of regulations

Specific requirements for the publication of new regulations are laid down in the Publication Act (*Bekendmakingswet*). All new legislation is placed on the Internet[7] after enactment by the parliament. Beyond this, ministries may make their own arrangements to provide greater accessibility to their regulations. Announcements of new regulations have to be published in the "*Staatscourant*".

There are specific provisions to facilitate access to regulations by the business community. New and upcoming regulations (those that have been approved by the cabinet) with effects on business (ministries must explain this in "plain Dutch") are published on the central business portal. The website provides links to more extensive descriptions of the changes in policy and the related regulations. The system covers primary laws, orders in council and ministerial regulations. Visitors to the website can choose between the Internet, e-mail, chat and the telephone for receiving information, which is sector specific. As part of the implementation of the EU Services Directive, there are plans to develop the portal into a single point of contact,[8] and to link central government information with that of local levels of government.

Common Commencement Dates (CCDs) are currently being set up.[9] Starting from 1 January 2009, two CCDs per year will be introduced, with a minimum implementation period of three months for all acts and orders in council directly relevant for businesses and organisations. Information will continue to be provided on relevant websites, and with timely and clear information on the development of draft regulations and their immediate effect on companies and institutions. These principles will be included in the Instructions for Legislation. The cabinet will examine in 2009 whether the CCD concept can be expanded to other types of legislation.[10]

Notes

1. Procedures for rule-making (Chapter 5); codification (Chapter 6); appeals (Chapter 7).
2. For more, see the 1999 OECD report.
3. They include some representative bodies such as consumer and banking associations.
4. Government of the Netherlands, Legislation in Perspective, p. 29, (English version).
5. Pre-publication of regulatory proposals and an invitation to comment from all members of the public.
6. *www.antwoordvoorbedrijven.nl.* The website is set up to answer questions from entrepreneurs, not only on topics relating to regulatory burdens, but also on bottlenecks experienced in their daily management of issues related to doing business. Entrepreneurs can e mail their questions, they can call the back office, but also have the opportunity to chat with the people of the back office. Through chatting they can receive immediate answers to their questions while sitting behind their computer. Also linked to the website is a suggestion box where entrepreneurs & businesses can ask questions about unclear or incompatible legislation, red tape/regulatory burden etc. Experts from the ministries have to explain the legislation and, if needed, find solutions. These suggestions can also be done via e-mail, chatting and telephone. The objective of the suggestion box is to explain legislation and give insight in to the legal requirements for a particular business, to find solutions and to improve communication between government and businesses.
7. *www.overheid.nl.*
8. *Dienstenrichtlijn.*
9. The purpose of CCDs is to help business plan for new regulation and to increase awareness of the introduction of new or changed requirements. By reducing to two dates each year, for example, on which new regulation may be started, it is hoped that increased awareness by businesses of new or changed obligations will result in improved compliance levels.

10. Ministerial regulations and policy regulations of implementing bodies and autonomous administrative authorities, because these regulations may have significant consequences for business processes and internal organisations. National legislation that has direct relevance to citizens and professionals and to national legislation that has direct relevance to local and regional authorities. Local and regional regulations, consultation with the Association of Netherlands Municipalities.

Chapter 4

The development of new regulations

Predictable and systematic procedures for making regulations improve the transparency of the regulatory system and the quality of decisions. These include forward planning (the periodic listing of forthcoming regulations), administrative procedures for the management of rule-making, and procedures to secure the legal quality of new regulations (including training and guidance for legal drafting, plain language drafting, and oversight by expert bodies).

Ex ante impact assessment of new regulations is one of the most important regulatory tools available to governments. Its aim is to assist policy makers in adopting the most efficient and effective regulatory options (including the "no regulation" option), using evidence-based techniques to justify the best option and identify the trade-offs involved when pursuing different policy objectives. The costs of regulations should not exceed their benefits, and alternatives should also be examined. However the deployment of impact assessment is often resisted or poorly applied, for a variety of reasons, ranging from a political concern that it may substitute for policy making (not true-impact assessment is a tool that helps to ensure a policy which has already been identified and agreed is supported by effective regulations, if they are needed), to the demands that it makes on already hard pressed officials. There is no single remedy to these issues. However experience around the OECD shows that a strong and coherent focal point with adequate resourcing helps to ensure that impact assessment finds an appropriate and timely place in the policy and rule making process, and helps to raise the quality of assessments.

Effective consultation needs to be an integral part of impact assessment. Impact assessment processes have – or should have – a close link with general consultation processes for the development of new regulations. There is also an important potential link with the measurement of administrative burdens (use of the Standard Cost Model technique can contribute to the benefit-cost analysis for an effective impact assessment).

The use of a wide range of mechanisms, not just traditional "command and control" regulation, for meeting policy goals helps to ensure that the most efficient and effective approaches are used. Experience shows that governments must lead strongly on this to overcome inbuilt inertia and risk aversion. The first response to a problem is often still to regulate. The range of alternative approaches is broad, from voluntary agreements, standardisation, conformity assessment, to self regulation in sectors such as corporate governance, financial markets and professional services such as accounting. At the same time care must be taken when deciding to use "soft" approaches such as self regulation, to ensure that regulatory quality is maintained.

An issue that is attracting increasing attention for the development of new regulations is risk management. Regulation is a fundamental tool for managing the risks present in society and the economy, and can help to reduce the incidence of hazardous events and their severity. A few countries have started to explore how rule-making can better reflect the need to assess and manage risks appropriately.

Assessment and recommendations

Ex ante impact assessment of new regulations

Although impact assessment has been established a long time, there is widespread agreement that the current process is in practice unsatisfactory, weak and ineffective. There is also considerable common ground as to what needs fixing. Nearly all of those interviewed by the OECD peer review team[1] expressed dissatisfaction with current impact assessment processes. Issues raised included the fact that impact assessment comes too late in the decision-making process to have any effect on outcomes, inadequate consultation, lack of transparency, failure to take into account benefits as well as costs, and the need to define a clear methodological approach balancing qualitative and quantitative analysis. There is an overemphasis on business costs defined fairly narrowly, and an under emphasis on alternatives to regulation (despite the efforts of the Ministry of Justice), benefits, non business impacts, consultation, and on support and quality control, which is fragmented and ineffective. There is little appreciation of the importance of evidence-based, cost-benefit analysis and other methodologies[2] for effective impact assessment. An analysis by the Proposed Legislation Desk (the institutional focal point of the process) shows that a considerable number of proposals are not sufficiently clear about the likely effects. Many of these issues had already been raised in the OECD's 1999 report, which drew specific attention to the need for effective quantification, the need to consider alternatives, and the need to consult (Box 4.1). There has been progress on some fronts since then, notably the quantification of administrative burdens for business, but not enough to generate an effective approach.

Box 4.1. Recommendation and comments from the 1999 OECD report: Impact assessment

- Improve the contribution of impact assessment (RIA) to good regulatory decisions by increasing methodological rigour, including adoption of a benefit-cost test; expanding it to incorporate detailed consideration of alternatives; and integrating RIA with consultation processes.

The Dutch RIA programme is in some ways strong. It applies to both primary and subordinate regulation, is targeted toward major regulation, and includes a highly developed and well-resourced system of assistance for ministries from co-ordinating agencies. Changes made since 1994 to the RIA system significantly improved its potential to contribute to regulatory quality. For example, targeting of RIA requirements to only the most significant regulations concentrated limited resources to their highest value in improving the cost-efficiency of regulations.

In particular, provision of significant resources through the help desk function is innovative and worthy of consideration by other OECD countries. Creation of a dedicated budget to fund analysis can help to overcome agency reluctance to divert resources to RIA, as can access to dedicated statistical resources from the help desk. The use of three co-ordinating departments to ensure that various aspects of regulatory quality are properly considered is another promising practice.

Yet the RIA programme has not been very effective in producing reliable data that can increase the cost-efficiency of regulatory decisions. OECD best practices suggest that three key steps are needed to improve its effectiveness: *i)* increase methodological rigour by providing training, written guidance, and minimum analytical standards including a requirement for benefit-cost tests to line ministries; *ii)* expand RIA to incorporate detailed consideration of alternatives; *iii)* ensure greater public scrutiny through integrating RIA with consultation processes.

First, the *degree of quantification* of regulatory benefits and costs remains low. Training and guidance for policy staff in the ministries would be a useful step, and adoption of standard minimum requirements such as quantitative analysis of direct costs of compliance through tools such as the Canadian Business Impact Test. Adoption of an explicit benefit-cost principle, as is currently being considered, would sharply improve the quality of regulatory decisions. The practical and conceptual difficulties of a formal benefit-cost analysis suggests that a step-by-step approach is needed in the Netherlands, in which the RIA programme is gradually improved, integrating both qualitative and quantitative elements of the analysis, so that over time it better supports application of the benefit-cost principle.

Second, the usefulness of RIA in promoting use of cost-effective policy tools would be significantly enhanced by a formal requirement that *feasible alternatives* be analysed and compared with the regulatory proposal. *MDW* does not appear to have had a significant impact in the rate of adoption of alternative policy instruments. While the performance of the Netherlands is relatively good with respect to use of innovative instruments, the use of environmental covenants, while still growing, does not appear to have accelerated as a result of actions taken under *MDW*. More rigorous assessment of alternatives should help identify a wider range of areas where they are the better choice.

The effectiveness of both of these strategies would be enhanced by *integration of RIA with consultation processes*. Publication of RIA through a procedure that required regulators to respond to comments from affected parties would enable consultation to function more effectively as a means of cost-effective information gathering, and thereby improve the information needed for good RIA. Access to RIA would also improve the quality of consultation by permitting the public to react to more concrete information. Such integration should, however, be carefully designed so that additional delays to the policy process are not introduced.

There is concern to control new regulations more effectively. Many stakeholders expressed an underlying concern at the need to control more effectively the burdens that are likely to arise from the flow of new regulations. Some interviewees made the important point that reforming governments – the Netherlands has carried out recent major recent reforms of its health and education sectors – are bound to generate significant new regulation, the effects of which need to be controlled.

At the same time, there does not appear to be a coherent view of how a strengthened impact assessment system might be structured, and no clear vision seems to have emerged from the work of officials to give shape to a new system. For the past two years, a group of officials has been examining ways of improving the process. Despite some useful elements (examining alternatives, web-based consultation) it seems unlikely that these proposals will give rise to an effective, integrated process with real buy-in across government, as the work is mainly promoted by one ministry (Justice) and no clear plan for a new process has yet emerged.

A new approach needs to be developed. The government needs to develop and promote a clear vision and integrated approach to impact assessment, which sets out what impact assessment is for and how it can contribute to stronger, more effective, evidence based policy-making, ensures that new regulations are fit for purpose, and conveys the message that the government understands the importance of bringing new regulations under control. The significant common ground that appears to exist over what is wrong now needs to be translated into a new strategy emphasising the central place that impact assessment has in the policy making process.

Recommendation 4.1. The Netherlands should develop a new strategy, structures and processes for the *ex ante* impact assessment of new regulations, taking account of the more detailed proposals set out below.

Responsibility for carrying impact assessments should remain with the individual ministries, framed by strong central supervision and quality control. Effective supervision and quality control is crucial to the success of an impact assessment process. The Netherlands rightly emphasise the responsibility of individual ministries. However, the current institutional structures for overseeing impact assessment are weak and have fallen into disuse. For example, the Proposed Legislation Desk appears to be increasingly sidelined (according to interviews with the OECD peer review team), does not have a sufficiently high standing in government, and provides advice rather direction.

Recommendation 4.2. A considerably more authoritative form of the Proposed Legislation Desk at official level should be established, reporting directly to the Ministerial Steering Group on Better Regulation chaired by the Prime Minister. This unit, which could be developed on the basis of the current officials' group that supports the Ministerial Steering Group, would have the functions of issuing and updating the relevant guidelines, providing advice and support for ministries in the development of impact assessments, and monitoring the quality of impact assessments, as well as advising ministers directly on the development of the process and the performance of ministries. Consideration should be given to whether the Steering Group should have a formal gatekeeper role for significant new regulatory proposals before they are submitted to the Cabinet (this could be a formal 'sign off', or referral back to the relevant Ministry for more analysis). ACTAL should be considered for an external oversight role, building on its current responsibilities for providing advice to the Cabinet.

Effective training and guidance need to be in place. Officials will need to be trained in the new approach and especially, in the application of the new methodology. The current guidance lacks a sharp edge, and does not cover Cost-Benefit analysis or any of the methodologies for quantification. The cultural changes required, particularly in terms of ensuring that senior management is on board, are as important as the development of technical expertise and this will also need attention. Recently, training on regulatory management techniques, including *ex ante* impact assessment and regulatory burden management, has been developed by the Finance ministry and ACTAL in conjunction with the Interior and Economic Affairs Ministries. In 2008, training was also given to employers of the legal agency of the House of Representatives, in the context of reducing the administrative burdens of amendments made by the parliament.

Box 4.2. Methodological issues for consideration and incorporation into new guidance and training

This needs to cover how to:

- Identify the underlying problems and (multiple) cause-effect relations.
- Link the policy objective and the mechanism chosen to deliver it in a way that allows identification of benefits and costs.
- Apply cost-benefit analysis (how to use market price data, stated and revealed preference analysis, analyse complex and indirect costs, discount rates plus guidance for how to deal with

situations where quantification is difficult/ impossible).

- Deal with distributional effects, benefit transfers, costs to government, producer/ consumer transfers, effects on different-sized firms changes between consumer/ producer surpluses.
- Deal with uncertainty, including sensitivity analysis, compliance rates.
- Use cost-effectiveness if cost-benefit measurement is too difficult (*e.g.* same benefit compared with difference means to bring it about).
- Establish a baseline scenario, the importance of a baseline measurement (the do-nothing option and how to calculate based on data, trends and economic analysis).
- Investigate unintended consequences, notably the risk-risk trade-off.*

* The so called risk-risk trade paradox refers to the situation in which efforts to manage one type of risk generates countervailing and potentially more relevant risks.

Recommendation 4.3. Training should be developed further to cover the overall process and to encourage the development of expertise in evidence-based policy making. There should also be specialised training on applying the methodology, drawing on support from economists as necessary (given that many officials are not economists by training). Methodology should be incorporated into authoritative step-by-step guidance for officials, which should also make clear the responsibilities of the various decision makers through the process (ministers, officials, the ministerial Steering Group, the supporting officials' group, officials themselves).

Methodological rigour is essential and most obviously achieved by cost/benefit analysis, but a quality dimension is equally important. The Netherlands, through its development and promotion of the Standard Cost Model for administrative burdens, already has the benefit of a culture that is used to quantitative methods, and quantification is a fundamental pillar for evidence-based policy-making. The methodology should therefore have a strong quantitative element, drawing inspiration from the experiences of other OECD countries that are already applying quantification (such as the US, UK, Australia). It should also incorporate a strong qualitative aspect, supported by multi-criteria analysis, not least to capture future benefits that may be difficult to monetise. It is important that benefits as well as costs are drawn out, as this is about Better Regulation, not deregulation.

Recommendation 4.4. A clear methodology with a quantity/quality balance should be established.

A single integrated, standardised process will help to give impact assessment the focus it needs to be adopted by ministries. Current separate processes need to be integrated into a single process which regroups the different assessments and legal quality tests. This standard process should be adopted across government. The format for presenting the new integrated impact assessment should be standardised, and kept simple and clear, so that it is comprehensible - the rationale for action and key conclusions of the impact assessment should be readily understood by decision makers as well as other stakeholders including the general public. Recourse to annexes for technical details would support the accuracy of the reported analysis. A staged approach to the process is needed, as now, but institutionally stronger. This would make it clear when, early in the policy development process, impact assessments need to be started, developed and updated, taking account of the need for efforts to be proportional, *i.e.* distinguishing between proposals that merit a full-impact assessment and others which need less attention. The current process generally only covers primary laws and orders in council. Consideration should be given to extending impact assessment to other regulations that are likely to be important for Better Regulation.

Recommendation 4.5. Establish a single integrated process for impact assessment across government, which includes a simple format, the stages of the process with the emphasis on starting early, and a clear and comprehensive definition of the regulations covered.

The EU and local dimensions to the development of regulations need attention. There is no reference to EU regulations in the current guidance and the EU dimension needs to be addressed. There is an equally important link to the local level, which has raised the issue of impacts on local government of centrally adopted regulations.

Recommendation 4.6. Ensure that the EU and local dimensions are effectively covered in the new process.

Consultation, which is not covered at all in the current process, needs to be addressed. Consultation needs to be a formal part of the impact assessment development process and engage all potential stakeholders. Broadly-based consultation (including on the web, building on the Internet pilot for consultation on new regulations that has been launched recently) should start early to give stakeholders the opportunity to comment on proposals before it is too late to influence the outcome, including the possibility of alternatives to regulation. Public consultation on draft impact assessments promotes the sharing of information and expertise, which enriches the draft and encourages ownership.

Recommendation 4.7. Impact assessment reports should be published on ministry websites, as well as the website of the lead supervisory authority, both at an appropriate drafting stage, and when finalised. Those who have contributed to consultation should be advised of the impact assessment's publication, and where important comments have been made, given feedback on how the comments were used (or an explanation of why they were not used). The views of the external oversight body should also be made public. Efforts should be made to ensure that the non-business community (those who may not have such as strong voice such as citizens and consumer advocacy bodies) are engaged with the process. [3]

Ex post evaluation also needs to be built into the new process. Feedback to the government on the effectiveness of the impact assessment process should be built in from the start, as part of the new strategy. There are several options for securing this, which are not mutually exclusive. They include giving ACTAL a role in ex post evaluation (building on its role of advice to the cabinet on regulatory burdens); annual reports to the parliament; tracking the development of new regulations; and last but least, encouraging the Netherlands Court of Audit (NCA) to carry out audits of the process. Audits by the NCA equivalents in some other countries, notably the UK, have made an important contribution to evaluating the effectiveness of policies to control the development of new regulations, including impact assessment.

Recommendation 4.8. Consideration should be given to the best way of arranging systematic *ex post* evaluation of the impact assessment process. The Ministry of Justice should be encouraged in its work to track the trends in development of new regulations.

Alternatives to regulations

The Ministry of Justice's efforts to draw attention to consideration of alternatives to regulation need support and further development, including and not least as part of an enhanced impact assessment process. Regulation may not be the only option. Before it is too late, the process should include consideration of alternative approaches to achieving desired regulatory outcomes. The significant efforts that were started over a decade ago in the use of alternatives need to be given a renewed impetus. The Ministry of Justice has issued a number of relevant documents and these now need to be made operational. An effective approach might examine the consequences of several different options, including an alternative to "command and control" regulation, and the "do-nothing" option. Guidance should be developed on the appropriate use of alternatives (such as non-legislative action, exemptions, principles-based rather than rule-based approaches, and outcome standards rather than process standards).

Recommendation 4.9. As already recommended in the 1999 OECD report (Box 4.3), the consideration of alternatives needs to be clearly and firmly anchored into a revitalised impact assessment process.

Box 4.3. Recommendation and comments from the 1999 OECD report: Alternatives

- Further encourage the use of cost-effective alternative policy instruments by developing operational guidance for ministries.

A requirement that analysis of alternatives currently required by the Directives on Legislation be documented and subjected to public scrutiny through the RIA process could stimulate genuine comparisons of the benefits and costs of various approaches. However, policy makers are likely to require assistance in the identification of suitable alternative policy tools. Operational guidance on the characteristics and use of alternative approaches should be developed for use by the line ministries.

Background

General context

The structure of regulations in the Netherlands

Box 4.4. The structure of Dutch regulations

Hierarchy of laws and regulations

Primary laws. These are for the most part initiated by the government and enacted by the parliament.[4] Primary laws may delegate powers to make secondary regulations to the government (royal decrees or orders in council), or directly to a minister (ministerial regulations).

Example: The *Zorgverzekeringswet* (Health Insurance Act) contains an obligation for every Dutch citizen to take out health insurance, as well as rules on the content, pricing and application for insurance companies offering those insurance.

Royal decrees (orders in council). These are made by the government under powers delegated by a primary law.

Example: The *Zorgverzekeringsbesluit* (Health Insurance Decree) develops several aspects of the obligations contained in the Health Insurance Act that are subject to frequent changes, so that regulation or those aspects by means of an act of the parliament would be too time consuming.

Ministerial regulations. These are made by individual ministers under powers delegated by a primary law. They are mainly used for technical matters and administrative procedures.

Example: The *Zorgverzekeringsregeling* (ministerial regulation on health insurance) contains provisions of a technical nature that may need to be changed faster than would be possible by an order in council.

Regulations made by agencies (e.g. financial, telecoms, health and safety). Agencies can make their own regulations under powers granted by primary laws. But these are unusual.

Example: The *Nederlandse Zorgautoriteit* (Dutch Health Authority) is charged with supervising and regulating several aspects of the services offered by health providers. In order to improve public transparency with respect to the performance of health providers, it has issued a *Regeling publicatie wachttijden somatische zorg* (regulation on the publication of waiting periods for somatic treatments). This regulation obliges health providers to offer information about the average waiting periods for their clients.

Regulations made by municipalities and provinces. General acts for municipalities and provinces give their councils powers to enact legislation – by-laws or ordinances – on matters for which they have exclusive competence ("household" matters). Provincial ordinances must not conflict with existing national legislation, and municipal ordinances must not conflict with the ordinances of the provinces to which they are attached. Municipalities and provinces may also make regulations under powers delegated by a primary law.

Trends in the production of new regulations

The Ministry of Justice has recently established a monitoring system for central government regulations in force, starting with a quantitative analysis carried out in 2004 of regulations in force since 1975. Monitoring since then has picked up the total number of laws, royal decrees and ministerial regulations in force at the beginning of each year. There is not, as yet, any separate monitoring of the number of new regulations or amendments to existing regulations each year, although this is planned (it is estimated that there are some 500 new central government regulations each year). Between 2004 and 2008 the number of central government regulations in force declined, levelling off from 2007 onwards. The most significant fall was in the number of ministerial regulations.

Figure 4.1. Trends in the number of central government regulations in force at the start of each year

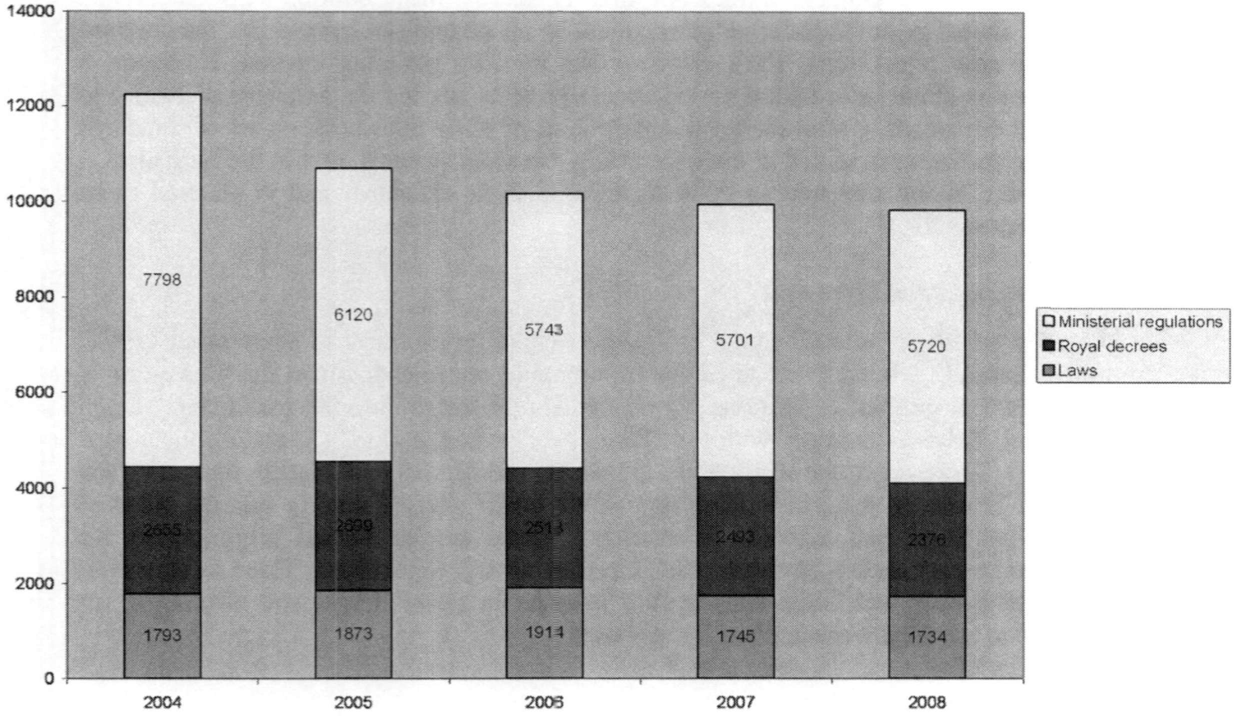

Source: Dutch government.

Processes for making new regulations

The law making process

Box 4.5. The Dutch law-making process[5]

Proposals for legislation are agreed by cabinet.

They go to the Council of State for scrutiny as to whether they are compatible with other laws and treaties (the Constitution, international treaties such as the European Convention on Human Rights, and European law (or, in the case of a draft order in Council, statutory law). The Council also considers proposed legislation from a wider angle: whether it is a "good" law that will serve the interests of citizens.

The proposal then goes to the monarch for signature (a formality), before it is tabled before the House of Representatives. The advice of the Council of State as well as an explanatory memorandum (purpose and contents) is attached to draft bills.

The bill is subject to scrutiny by the relevant parliamentary standing committee. The committee may arrange a hearing, and make enquiries, or request a briefing by government Advisory bodies such as the Central Planning Office, the Central Bureau of Statistics, or external experts. A report is drawn up and sent to all members of the House, and to the government. The government responds to this report.

The draft bill then goes to plenary for debate. Amendments may be tabled by members of the House during the debate. The bill – amended or otherwise – is then sent to the Senate.

Once passed by the Senate, the bill is returned to the monarch for formal signature, alongside the signature of the responsible minister. The act is then signed by the Minister of Justice, who arranges for it to be published in the Bulletin of Acts and Decrees.

Forward planning

Beyond the very general framework that is set by the Coalition Agreement and subsequent annual policy/legislative plans, there is no centralised system for the forward planning of new regulations. Each ministry has its own planning system. However, a growing need to share information on legislative projects has led the Ministry of Justice to develop – in co-operation with the legal departments of other ministries – a set of standards for planning and control, aimed at interoperability between systems, and in the long term, a shared system. Work will start in 2009 to develop these standards and is planned to be completed before 2011.

Administrative procedures

There is no single administrative procedure regulation as exists in some other OECD countries. Instead, general procedures for rule-making are laid down in the Constitution, and elaborated in internal regulations within the administration and the parliament.[6] Legal drafters must, however, comply with the "Directives on Legislation" (*Aanwijzigingen voor regelgeving*). These are a set of rules, developed by the Ministry of Justice, agreed by the cabinet and issued by the Prime Minister, which cover general quality criteria, rules of procedure and legal and editorial instructions. There are no formal requirements for ministries to consult each other in the development of new regulations. There is, however, an incentive to carry out some consultation in order to avoid delays and blockages, for example when a draft goes to cabinet for approval.

Legal quality

Ministries are responsible for drafting legislation in their policy field. Each ministry has a legal department in which bills are drafted. Since 2001, the Academy for Legislation offers a two-year postdoctoral training "on the job" programme for legal drafters, as well as ongoing training. Postdoctoral training is only offered to selected new legal drafters. Legal drafters who are already employed within government are not required to follow the programme. Since 2001, most legal drafters have followed some form of training with the Academy.

The Ministry of Justice has overall responsibility for legal quality, and a quality framework has been in place since 1991. The definition of legal quality, compared with the definition used in many other countries, is quite broad. The Ministry of Justice considers the likely effectiveness of a proposed regulation in relation to policy goals, including whether alternatives to regulation would be more effective. The ministry also develops and disseminates guidance on legislation and the legislative process, and provides advice and support on the transposition of EU regulations. It offers a central contact point and runs a specialised website.

The ministry is also, more strategically, active in developing and refining policy on the legislative process. Its most recent policy document, "Trust in Legislation" (*Vertrouwen in wetgeving*) was sent to the parliament in November 2008. The document stresses the importance of having a realistic view about what can be achieved with legislation, and the need to consider the costs and burdens of unnecessary or overly complicated regulation. The government should also put trust in, and leave room for other (civil) institutions and control mechanisms when considering the necessity of legislation. In the document several projects are announced with the purpose to improve the quality of the legislation and the legislation process, such as the development of an integrated regulatory impact assessment structure for policy and regulation, the creation of a clearing house for evaluation of regulations and the promotion of the use of ICT in making legislation.

The current quality framework covers six criteria:

- legal compliance (is a proposed regulation lawful, does it obey legal principles *e.g.* as regards the Constitution, European law?);
- effectiveness and efficiency (is a proposed regulation likely to be effective and efficient?);
- subsidiarity and proportionality (is a proposed regulation useful and necessary?);
- feasibility and enforceability (is a proposed regulation practicable and enforceable?);
- co-ordination with other regulations in the same field / at the same level (is a proposed regulation well co-ordinated and in harmony with related regulations?); and
- simplicity, clarity and accessibility (is a proposed regulation simple, clear and transparent?).

The Ministry of Justice scrutinises all draft central government legislation against these criteria (the legislative test) before they are submitted to the cabinet for approval.

Ex ante impact assessment of new regulations

Policy on impact assessment

Ex ante impact analysis (impact assessment) has a long history in the Netherlands. Some form of impact assessment has been required since 1985, via the Directives on Regulation. The early requirements were ineffective, consisting of a very general questionnaire that only sought to identify side effects of proposed regulations (*i.e.* what might be overlooked), rather than a careful weighing of the whole impact. Impact assessment was overhauled in 1994-95 as part of the then new cabinet's policy on regulatory reform. It stressed co-operation between three ministries – Justice, Economic Affairs and Environment – to improve the quality of analysis, and established a central help desk (the Proposed Legislation Desk that still exists today), shared by the three ministries.

A new and mandatory process was agreed in 2002 by the cabinet. It covers not one but several distinct impact assessments:

- *A Business Impact Assessment (BIA).* This is intended to show the effects of proposed legislation for the business community. It consists of eight questions. The guidance notes the importance of quantification, without going into the detail. The process is directly linked to the business regulatory burden reduction programme. Data generated by the latter is re-used for this impact assessment.
- *An Environmental Impact Assessment (EA).* This identifies the intended and unintended effects on the environment, for example on energy usage, mobility and waste treatment.
- *A Practicability and Enforcement Assessment (P&E).* This facilitates identification of the effects of proposed legislation for implementing and enforcement authorities, including ministries, agencies, but also authorities such

as the police, Public Prosecutor's Office and judiciary. Again, the same broad approach and guidance is offered as for BIA. The Table of Eleven checklist is appended (see Chapter 6).

- *Cost-Benefit Analysis (CBA).* This is mentioned separately from the other impact assessments. It is intended to clarify the financial consequences of new legislation for the "community".

Impact assessments – as well as the other legal checks on proposed legislation (see section above on legal quality) – are only mandatory for central government primary laws, orders in council and amendments to them. Budget laws and laws initiated by the parliament are not covered. The process also does not generally apply to decrees or ministerial regulations, nor does it apply to the regulations issued by agencies, municipalities and provinces. If thought necessary, however, impact assessments may be performed on these forms of regulation.

There is considerable interest in the development of a stronger impact assessment process. The OECD peer review team were told by the Ministry of Justice that a consolidated and strengthened *ex ante* impact assessment process was under development, via a working group of legal drafters, in order to "enhance the consideration of alternatives, accountability and effects", with the aim of having the new approach operational by 2011. The approach will be staged – two pilots are proposed for spring 2009. It is not clear, however, how far the work has in reality progressed, as there are no documents yet available on the plans, and the OECD peer review team was not provided with any information on the outcome of discussions taking place in the legal working group.[7] The Regulatory Reform Group for its part also expressed keen interest in the development of a stronger impact assessment process, and asked the OECD team for advice on how this could be achieved, and what a strengthened impact assessment process should consist of.

Institutional framework

The initiating ministry is responsible for the overall quality of proposed legislation, and for developing the required impact assessments. It is supported and monitored by the Proposed Legislation Desk which may provide general help (for example, to identify sources of data), and which checks the quality of impact assessments. The Proposed Legislation Desk is operated jointly by the Regulatory Reform Group (Business Impact Assessment), the Ministry of the Environment (Environmental Assessment) and the Ministry of Justice (Practicability and Enforceability Assessment).

A guidance paper produced by the Proposed Legislation Desk[8] has been prepared for ministries. The guidance includes manuals for the first three impact assessments but not for cost-benefit analysis, as "it will not very often be necessary, and requires specific technical skills". Courses and lectures on impact assessment have been offered to ministries and other institutions involved in the legislative process (including as part of courses at the Academy of Legislation). Recently, training on regulatory management techniques, including *ex ante* impact assessment and regulatory burden management, has been developed by the Ministry of Finance and ACTAL in conjunction with the Ministry of Interior and the Ministry of Economic Affairs. In 2008, training was also given to employers of the legal agency of the House of Representatives, in the context of reducing the administrative burdens of amendments made by the parliament on draft new legislation.[9]

Process and methodology

There are no standard or compulsory analytical methods. The contents of the impact assessments are "form free". The emphasis remains, as identified in the 1999 OECD report, on capturing side effects rather than a consolidated weighing up of overall impacts.

The process for carrying out impact assessments is expected to follow two stages (the guidance recommends starting as early as possible):

- *Quick scan.* The initiating ministry must perform a quick scan to examine whether the proposed regulation (or amendment to an existing regulation) is desirable or necessary (if a proposal is not expected to have any significant impacts, there is no scope for alternatives, and it is a mandatory EU regulation, the quick scan does not need to be performed). The scan considers whether substantial consequences are likely in respect of the issues covered by the different impact assessments (business, environment etc), and whether a cost-benefit analysis is needed. The Proposed Legislation Desk checks the ministry's proposals including its choice of impact assessments to be performed.

- *Performance of impact assessments.* External expert support is mandatory in some cases (for example Statistics Netherlands for the business impact). Once the impact assessments have been completed, they are submitted to the Ministry of Justice for the legislative test (see section above on legal quality). At the same time, the Ministry of Justice commissions a review of the completed impact assessments from the relevant ministries (RRG for the BIA, Environment for the EA and itself for the P&E).

The results of all these tests are brought together by the Ministry of Justice into a report which states "approval or disapproval". If agreement cannot be reached with the responsible ministry, the report of the Ministry of Justice is attached to the proposal that goes to the cabinet.

If proposed legislation affects administrative burdens, it must also be submitted to ACTAL, the independent advisory body on Better Regulation. These burdens are expected to be quantified and ACTAL will base its recommendations on these figures. ACTAL provides written advice to the cabinet on this. In 2003, 2004 and 2005, ACTAL reviewed a total of 730 proposed regulations and gave a formal report in 198 cases (half of these in 2005). According to the latest numbers, ACTAL worked on 198 files in 2008 and published advice in 47 cases.[10] The reports are divided into four categories: ACTAL can approve the proposed regulation with no further comments, approve it conditionally (stating necessary changes), reject it conditionally, or fully reject it. Only in seven cases has the proposed regulation been fully rejected, while full or conditional approval is most common.

The Council for the Judiciary (see Annex A) may also be asked for its advice concerning the likely impact of a regulation for the administration of justice. Its role is set out in an appendix to the guidance paper. An official request for advice must be submitted when the regulation is under development. Its advice will cover the administrative costs for the judicial "chain", to be included in the overall expected financial costs. It may also be consulted informally. If it provides advice, this must be incorporated into the report of the Ministry of Justice to the cabinet.

Public consultation and communication

Impact assessments are not available to the general public, apart what goes into the Explanatory Memorandum to the parliament, attached to draft bills. There is no formal requirement to consult as part of the process. Consultation is not mentioned in the guidance.

Alternatives to regulation

A main goal of the legislative quality policy of the Ministry of Justice is to develop and encourage the use of alternatives to regulation. Since the 1990s a broad range of white papers and checklists have been established, concerning for example the use of normalisation and certification, covenants, duties of care, general rules as an alternative for permits, tradable permits, contributions to public services.

Risk-based approaches

The Netherlands have been working to develop risk-based approaches in the development of regulations. New legislation is often based on risk analyses and a focus on activities relating to businesses as well as citizens with a higher risk profile. The use of risk-based approaches however, is not yet systematic. To stimulate its development, the RRG and REAL have been encouraging a dialogue to discuss risk-based regulation and the mechanisms that generate burdensome regulations. Part of this discussion has focused on (dis)trust as an issue which encourages unnecessarily burdensome legislation. The RRG and REAL want to find out how to use trust as a steering instrument for "light regulatory" governance, the shape this should take and the regulatory areas or business sectors in which pilots can be started up. It is seeking to bring together various stakeholders; policy makers, academics, politicians and business representatives. There are two different approaches;

- A fundamental track to find out which "factor" is needed to prevent the regulatory mechanism from increasing distrust and regulatory burdens.
- A second track to search for and organise countervailing powers to slow down and reverse the cycle of increasing distrust and regulatory burdens.

The goal of this discussion is to develop an operational mechanism which can be put into force as soon as possible to counter the continuing development of regulatory burden mechanisms. A round table discussion is planned for May 2009. Further analyses and a policy approach are expected in October 2009.

Notes

1. Officials as well as external stakeholders.
2. Such as sensitivity analysis, and multicriterial analysis.
3. Citizen views should not just be confined to the citizen burden reduction programme. In any event there is an important link with the development of new regulations that may add to their burdens.

4. The lower house of the parliament also has the right to initiate legislation.

5. Primary laws and orders in council.

6. For example: *Aanwijzingen voor de regelgeving, Reglement van orde TK en EK, Reglement van orde voor de ministerraad.*

7. It made a request for information.

8. "Assessment of Proposed Legislation – explanatory notes, step-by-step plan, quick scan, manuals".

9. This followed the "*Blanksma Van den Heuvel and Smeets*" resolution by two spokespersons for Better Regulation.

10. The annual reports from 2006 and 2007 state: In 2006 there was advice on 58 proposals (total 58 + 194 = 252 files); in 2007 there was advice on 41 cases (total 41 + 160 files).

Chapter 5

The management and rationalisation of existing regulations

This chapter covers two areas of regulatory policy. The first is simplification of regulations. The large stock of regulations and administrative formalities accumulated over time needs regular review and updating to remove obsolete or inefficient material. Approaches vary from consolidation, codification, recasting, repeal, *ad hoc* reviews of the regulations covering specific sectors, and sun setting mechanisms for the automatic review or cancellation of regulations past a certain date.

The second area concerns the reduction of administrative burdens and has gained considerable momentum over the last few years. Government formalities are important tools to support public policies, and can help businesses by setting a level playing field for commercial activity. But they may also represent an administrative burden as well as an irritation factor for business and citizens, and one which tends to grow over time. Difficult areas include employment regulations, environmental standards, tax regulations, and planning regulations. Permits and licences can also be a major potential burden on businesses, especially SMEs. A lack of clear information about the sources of and extent of administrative burdens is the first issue for most countries. Burden measurement has been improved with the application by a growing number of countries of variants on the standard cost model (SCM) analysis to information obligations imposed by laws, which also helps to sustain political momentum for regulatory reform by quantifying the burden. [1]

A number of governments have started to consider the issue of administrative burdens inside government, with the aim of improving the quality and efficiency of internal regulation in order to reduce costs and free up resources for improved public service delivery. Regulation inside government refers to the regulations imposed by the state on its own administrators and public service providers (for example, government agencies or local government service providers). Fiscal restraints may preclude the allocation of increased resources to the bureaucracy, and a better approach is to improve the efficiency and effectiveness of the regulations imposed on administrators and public service providers.

The effective deployment of e-Government is of increasing importance as a tool for reducing the costs and burdens of regulation on businesses and citizens, as well as inside government.

Assessment and recommendations

Simplification of regulations

There is no systematic effort to consolidate or simplify the regulatory stock. As in other countries with well developed burden reduction programmes, simplification[2] is mainly a "derivative product" of the efforts to reduce administrative burdens (as for example in the review of regulatory clusters or related laws). As complexity accumulates over time in all areas of regulation, there is a need for more systematic "spring cleaning" at regular intervals. The OECD review team was told that the business community would welcome a "clean-up" of the existing law.

Administrative burden reduction for businesses[3]

Achievements have already been considerable by international standards, and the Netherlands' 2003- 2007 policy identified the main elements of a successful model which has been replicated elsewhere. The 2003-07 cabinet had a 25% net burden reduction target allocated across ministries, based on a carefully quantified baseline measurement, which it broadly achieved. As already recorded in the 2007 OECD/World Bank report, the Dutch model has been an inspiration to other countries, and the considerable investment made by successive Dutch governments since the 1990s has largely paid off. The success factors, as listed in that report, have been a combination of measurement (the SCM method for the measurement and mapping of burdens); setting a time bound quantitative target (divided among ministries); a strong inter-ministerial co-ordinating unit at the centre of government (the RRG and its predecessor, IPAL); independent monitoring via the watchdog, ACTAL; link to the budget cycle; and not least, political support, helped by the narrow focus of the programme on administrative burdens which helped to avoid controversy. It is fair to note that the Netherlands may have had further to go than some other countries, in terms of the relative weight of administrative burdens as a proportion of GDP.[4] But this also means that the Netherlands was probably right to put particular emphasis in the last few years on this part of its Better Regulation strategy.

A new phase has opened up, with the establishment of an ambitious, broad- and well-designed new policy. This builds on key elements of the previous policy which have proved their worth (not least a reinforced institutional structure), as well as adding new aspects. The current cabinet has set a further 25% reduction target, based on a (largely) new baseline measurement. The current action plan captures a number of important new issues, as well as addressing weaknesses in the original methodology. This reflects the price paid for being a first mover with no role model to follow, but is also testimony to the fact that the Netherlands is remarkably open to learning from its own and others' experiences, as well as taking advice from independent experts, which it calls in regularly. Among the issues which are being vigorously addressed in this new phase are the extension of the programme to cover burdens at the subnational levels of government (still very unusual in OECD countries); addressing the burdens raised by enforcement; a renewed attack on the issue of licences; the development of an *ex post* evaluation framework; the establishment of common commencement dates for new regulations; and not least, the development of the SCM methodology to cover qualitative as well as quantitative aspects and to broaden the definition to cover all compliance costs.

A substantial update and broadening of the programme was necessary, in order to sustain progress towards a new target, but this also raises new challenges. The programme has until recently enjoyed broad support, politically, within ministries, as well as from outside stakeholders. This now looks more vulnerable. As already noted in the 2007 OECD/World Bank report, a politically neutral programme is no longer an option. Proposals for further reform, if they are based on a broader definition of compliance costs, are likely to be politically more sensitive and engage more vested interests. The report also underlined the importance at this stage of having clear goals.

Box 5.1. Comments from the 2007 OECD/World Bank report

The 2007 OECD/World Bank report recommended that the programme be broadened to include a broader definition of compliance costs (among other issues), in order to sustain momentum. But it also drew attention to the need for a "very clear formulation of definitions and goals", including a "balance between protection and dynamism", and that it "may be necessary to re-evaluate the principle of political neutrality", as the price to pay for a broader approach on compliance costs. It further noted that "societal and/or economic optimal solutions can be contrary to special interests and ambitious simplification projects may at times have to disregard explicit opposition from stronger stakeholders".

The key stakeholders that matter for progress: Business, implementing ministries, and the parliament. Business is frustrated at what it considers to be slow progress and the failure to tackle issues that really matter from its perspective. The OECD peer review team also heard that there was discouragement, even resistance, within ministries with regard to the new target, based on a worry that it will not be easy to achieve, as many of the "low-hanging fruit" have been cleared off the trees. Even some of the remaining low-hanging fruit can raise unexpected problems.[5] The parliament for its part, whilst it takes a keen interest through the regular reports on general progress by the RRG, does not always seem prepared to turn this into specific backing for proposals that require legislative action, without which the new target will not be met.

Addressing business concerns: The government is taking the right direction with its expanded definition of compliance costs, and a new communication strategy which is well conceived. For a number of reasons, which are broadly shared with other countries at advanced stages in the deployment of burden reduction programmes, the Netherlands has been confronted with negative business reactions despite evident progress on a number of fronts. The reasons for this include time lags before promised results are delivered[6]; frustration at the scrapping of rules that were not complied with in the first place; and slowness in identifying and addressing key issues for business such as licences delivered by the local level.[7] The situation has not been helped by the redefinition of the baseline for the new target, which calculates that burdens are now only some EUR 10 billion compared with some EUR 16 billion in 2003 (the main reason being that information obligations to third parties are no longer part of the baseline). ACTAL underlined to the OECD peer review team that irritants as well as substantive regulatory changes must be addressed at this stage, as businesses do not readily distinguish between administrative burdens and other compliance costs. In short, it strongly supports a broader approach.

The government has reacted comprehensively to the concerns expressed by the business community. As well as the ongoing work to expand the scope of the programme with a methodology that includes irritants and broader compliance costs, and the quality of services, its new highly proactive communications strategy targets needs as identified by business rather than civil servants. This includes the establishment of the *Wientjes* Commission to be the voice of business (which seems to meet with general approval), and a wide range of tailored mechanisms to capture business interests as well as to communicate meaningful achievements (what the recipient wants to know, rather than what the civil servant thinks is interesting). The RRG's communication handbook underlines that concrete results must have been achieved before they are communicated. As the RRG put it, the strategy seeks to integrate communication into the actual process of regulatory management, rather than as a disconnected "add on" to explain what government is doing. It is too soon to give a view on the effectiveness of the strategy and regular evaluation will be important – as the government plans to do. The government needs to show results from the new approach fairly quickly if a positive business attitude is to be restored.

Recommendation 5.1. The government should evaluate regularly the effectiveness and results of its action plan and communication strategy (as it plans to do).

Encouraging ministries to deliver on the more demanding new target. Despite a strong underlying institutional structure, spearheaded by the RRG and ACTAL, there is a need for further support and strengthening of the framework in order to encourage ministries to deliver. The need for enhanced co-operation with "delivery" ministries and further culture change is acknowledged by the RRG. As in other countries, a judicious mix of carrots and sticks is needed. A priority should be to allocate each Ministry its own target. This will encourage real ownership of the programme where it is needed: within ministries rather than with the RRG. Carrots are important – ministries experiencing fatigue from years of efforts need encouragement. So are sticks, for which sanctions must be credible. The Netherlands has gone further than most other countries in linking achievements to the budget cycle. The reporting structure to the parliament is linked to the reporting cycle for the budget (with key documents to the parliament in September and May). This means that the round of budget negotiations with respective ministers is preceded by a round of bilateral talks about progress on their respective regulatory burden reduction programmes, allowing this –if necessary- to be discussed further in the budget talks. Consideration should also be given to making a link between achievements and performance appraisals (which would have both a carrot and stick effect). At the same time, ministries need to feel supported in their efforts to push through controversial proposals. This implies some hard choices and trade-offs, for which political support is required. The cabinet and the Steering Group for Better Regulation chaired by the Prime Minister have an important role to play in this regard.

Recommendation 5.2. The government should ensure that budgetary and performance sanctions (or rewards) are in place and are credible, to encourage meeting of targets. The Steering Group for Better Regulation needs to play a strong role in dealing with the more controversial proposals that will arise, settling trade-offs and providing collective political support under the aegis of the Prime Minister for the adoption of such proposals.

Extending the dialogue with the parliament to cover specific decisions that will require its approval. The parliament is already heavily engaged in the programme at a strategic level, with the regular reports that it gets from the cabinet via the RRG. There is a need to strengthen and clarify the link between these reports and the specific measures that come to the parliament for approval under the programme. Since the easier targets have been achieved, much of the new work, especially if it is based on an extended interpretation of compliance costs, may need to go through the parliament in order for regulations to be changed or adopted. Skilful piloting will be required. At the same time, although regular updates are essential to sustain parliamentary interest and general support, quarterly reports (even if two of these are short updates) seem excessive, detracting the RRG (which prepares the reports) from getting on with the substantive work of developing the programme.

Recommendation 5.3. The government should reduce the number of reports made to the parliament on the programme, from quarterly to half yearly, without reducing their substantive content. It should balance reporting with a consideration of how to strengthen the dialogue with key parliamentary committees in order to encourage a positive attitude to proposals for change under the programme. The RRG should also, as far as possible, encourage ministries to link related proposals into packages before they are put to the parliament, drawing attention to their contribution (where appropriate) to the main strategic objectives of the programme.

Administrative burden reduction for citizens, professionals in the public sector and inter-governmental administrative burdens

This is a well-designed policy which has been carefully developed and adapted to take account of experience in the first phase. The Ministry of Interior has developed a programme based on a careful review of what actually matters for citizens. As with the programme for the reduction of burdens on business, from which it was inspired, this project seeks to learn from previous experience (the first phase was acknowledged to be unsatisfactory), to identify the challenges that still need to be met. It makes extensive use of external experts in moving forward. Such openness and willingness to learn is an extremely positive aspect of the Netherlands' general approach to Better Regulation. Among a number of positive features of the project, the local level is engaged in the programme, and extensive use is made of ITC. Efforts are made to cover important aspects in the Netherlands geographical context, such as the needs of cross border workers. Considerable effort goes into promoting an EU level approach to the issues.

It is not, however, clear how real progress will be evaluated and measured under an approach which does not set any clear quantitative baseline and reduction target. Without this, it is likely to prove difficult to demonstrate that there have been improvements.

Recommendation 5.4. The government should consider how it can best give shape to a concrete target or targets, linked to a clear baseline that would enable stakeholders to assess progress.

There are considerable and possibly unexploited synergies, between the citizen, professionals and inter-governmental programme, and the business burden reduction programme. In a broad sense, the Ministry of Interior has learnt from the much longer standing business programme in developing the citizen programme. An element of friendly competition between programmes is also no bad thing. That said, there are numerous points of convergence. It is not clear how much co-operation exists already. These include an overlap in coverage, communication strategy, the use of ICT, a shared independent watchdog (ACTAL), and also the development of new qualitative as well as quantitative methodologies, some of which might have a shared interest for the two programmes.

Recommendation 5.5. The government should consider whether it would be helpful to reinforce links between the different programmes, and ensure that areas of common interest are addressed jointly.

Regulation inside government is already part of the programme of the Interior ministry but could be expanded. Part of this programme addresses regulation inside the administration, notably for professionals working in public services such as hospitals and schools. The aim is to free up time spent on administration so that services to citizens can be enhanced. Greater emphasis on addressing regulation inside government was already recommended by the 2007 OECD/World Bank report. With a planned cut of 25% in the civil service, development of this part of the programme could help to release resources as well as making a contribution to better service quality.

Recommendation 5.6. Consideration should be given to expanding the elements of the project that address regulation inside government.

Background

Simplification of regulations

Simplification is tackled mainly *ad hoc*, through the programme for the reduction of administrative burdens. In the 2003-07 programme, there was a substantial cleaning up of the Annual Accounts Act, as well as reviews of entire regulatory complexes (see below). The current programme includes "fundamental surveys", some of which will be based on a sector, issue or area of legislation.

Administrative burden reduction for businesses

Policy on administrative burden reduction for businesses

Pioneering work on a new approach[8]

The Netherlands were pioneers in the development of a measurement system for administrative burdens, originally labelled MISTRAL,[9] which gave rise to an international brand (the Standard Cost Model – SCM), that has been adopted by a growing number of countries in recent years. The roots of today's programme can be traced back to 1994, with the establishment of the *MDW* (*Marktwerking, Deregulering en Wetgevingskwaliteit*) programme which targeted the better functioning of markets, deregulation and legislative quality. A main aim of the *MDW* programme was the reduction of administrative burdens, to streamline regulations in order to return to "what is strictly necessary". The report of the *Slechte* Committee in 1999 confirmed the direction, proposing that progress was best made and politicisation avoided by giving the administrative burden reduction programme a relatively narrow focus. The establishment of ACTAL, the independent external watchdog for the programme, in 2001 marked an institutional milestone.

The 2003-07 programme

The period following the 2003 election saw a strengthening of this approach, with the establishment of a quantified baseline and reduction target, a link to the budget cycle, and a strengthened institutional support structure. Administrative burdens were defined as "the costs to business of complying with the information obligations resulting from government imposed regulations". The government set the objective of reducing burdens by 25% by the end of its term, relative to a 2003 baseline measurement of EUR 16.4 billion (3.6% of GDP). Overall, ministries met their targets.

Current policy (RRG, 2007)

Following the 2007 elections, an updated action plan has been put in place, based on the recommendations of the joint review conducted by the OECD and the World Bank in 2007. The current cabinet (2007-11) has expressed its goals for this period in the following terms:

"To reduce regulatory burdens perceptibly for business, the cabinet wants to see *less* annoyance for businesses from things that irritate them. The cabinet also aims to make things *simpler* for business – for instance, with faster and better service. Ultimately, by decreasing regulatory burden and making it easier for businesses to comply with the obligations imposed by government, there will be less regulatory burden in the *perception* of business."

The new strategy strengthens previous policies and adds some important new aspects. Specific targets have been set, to be achieved by the end of the current cabinet term in 2011:

- *A new target for the reduction of administrative burdens on business.* Administrative burdens will be reduced by a further 25% net by 2011, based on a (largely) new baseline measurement.

- *Lower compliance costs.* The SCM methodology is being developed to broaden the definition of compliance costs. Compliance costs of regulations will be reduced in those cases where the identified costs turn out to be disproportionately high for businesses in relation to the public interest served by these regulations.

- *Lower supervisory costs, via streamlined supervision and enforcement.* The aim is to reduce state supervision, with the participation of the national inspectorates, and in consultation with business representatives. The latter were consulted in the selection of a number of supervisory domains, for which the aim will be to reduce state supervision by an average of 25% per domain. A new measure, closely related to SCM, will be developed (the Measurement Model Supervisory Burden) to cover both the burden in itself, and the burden as it is experienced (perception).

- *Lower costs in relation to subsidies.* Many companies find this complex. The aim is to ensure that all existing national government subsidies have low management and implementation costs, whilst safeguarding their legitimacy.

- *Better service.* The objectives are more professional, client-oriented and faster provision of services to businesses, addressing inconsistencies in the interpretation of rules, lack of expertise, time delays, a digital counter for business, and agreements with local/regional authorities for service improvement.

- *Greater transparency.* Information provision to business will be improved. The aim is to convey as much business information as possible through a single channel. This includes the introduction of common commencement dates, and readable, comprehensible forms.

- *Ex post evaluation.* Development of a "clearing house for the evaluation of legislation" which will consolidate previous disaggregated efforts at evaluation in order to achieve a more systematic approach.

- *Simplification of permits.* Acceleration of the procedure for granting permits by combining licences and, where possible, by a broader application of the *lex silencio positivo* principle (see below).[10]

- *Addressing burdens linked to local and regional authorities, and EU-origin regulations.* The programme has been extended to cover burdens generated at local level, and there will be enhanced emphasis on dialogue with the EU (and other member states) to promote burden reduction at EU level. Central government and the local levels have agreed that there will be a local contribution to the 25% reduction target. A baseline "zero" measurement is currently being made of local burdens, based on a sample of 25 municipalities.

Institutional framework, guidance and support

A dual approach has been in place for some time and is a cornerstone of Dutch policy on administrative burden reduction. It consists of a dedicated unit of officials at the centre of government to support, monitor, and steer the process (the RRG, previously IPAL), and an independent advisory body (ACTAL). An overarching pillar is the overall responsibility of two core ministries for delivery of the programme. The RRG reports to the state secretaries for Finance and Economic Affairs and through them, to the cabinet via the Ministerial Steering Group for Better Regulation. The parliament is also directly engaged in the programme, at least at a strategic level, through the quarterly progress reports submitted to it by the RRG.

As in other OECD countries with burden reduction programmes, individual ministries are responsible for delivering their share of the overall target. RRG account managers keep in regular touch with each ministry over progress and to offer advice. ACTAL also offers technical advice and support. Ministries must follow detailed instructions on how and when to report on progress, linked to the budget cycle and their budget reports. This means that reporting to the parliament is linked to the reporting cycle of the budget (with key documents to the parliament in September and May). It also means that the round of budget negotiations with respective ministers is preceded by a round of bilateral talks about the progress on their respective regulatory burden reduction programmes, allowing this – if necessary – to be discussed further in the budget talks. The budget instructions contain specific obligations to report on administrative burden reductions.[11] Ministries are threatened with budget cuts if they fail to achieve their targets (though this has apparently not yet happened). Beyond the obvious disciplinary effect, the OECD peer review team were told that this clear link to the budget cycle has the advantage of encouraging decisions over how to finance burden reduction projects such as ICT investments.

Part of the current cabinet's new strategy has been to boost external institutional structures. There is a renewed emphasis on the role of ACTAL as watchdog and adviser. ACTAL will continue, as before, to monitor the quality of assessments, and it will boost its strategic advice to government. It will report back on progress to the cabinet in 2011. The *Wientjes* Commission (Box 5.2) is another significant development. This has been set up as a channel for businesses to communicate to government on the issues that matter to them, so as to focus the programme on the problems important to business itself (rather than those identified by civil servants). The work programme will be developed on an ongoing basis to meet this objective, incorporating suggestions from businesses. The *Wientjes* Commission has a strong ambassadorial function. This ambassadorial function of the group focuses on keeping the reduction of regulatory burdens high on the agenda, both at the government level and within the business community.

Box 5.2. The Business Regulatory Burdens Commission (*Commissie Regeldruk Bedrijven - Wientjes*)

This Commission (chaired by Bernard *Wientjes* who is also president of the Confederation of the Netherlands Industry and Employers (VNO-NCW), the largest employers' organisation in the Netherlands) was recently established to be the voice of business. The commission was set up for three years until mid 2011 as part of the government's efforts to ensure that the policy to tackle administrative burdens meets their needs. Its formal mission is defined thus: to ensure that the business community has the opportunity to put suggestions and ideas to the government, and to ensure that burden reductions are noticeable for business. The board is made up of nine officials from the business community, one mayor, the Secretary General of the Economic Affairs Ministry, the chairman of the Board of Inspections, and the chairman of the Social Insurance Board. It is supported by the RRG which provides the secretariat, as well as representatives from the business organisations. It has the following specific tasks:

- Assess government plans. Do they cover the right areas? Will measures have enough impact? This work is supported by business panels.
- Put fundamental issues on the agenda. Identify broader connections. Members can suggest themes, and then adopt one each. This might be supported by workshops or research, in co-operation with the RRG or others.
- Act as ambassador for administrative burden reduction. It can table issues both to the government and to the business community, and promote priorities. Supported by the RRG, it can show what the government has done, and invite new proposals.
- It is currently pursuing projects under the general banner of "from mistrust to trust": trust and permits, trust and supervision, societal risks, and the dynamics of legislation.

Methodology and process

The methodology is going through a substantial update:

- *New baseline measurement for administrative burdens.* This is based on a selective analysis of the 2003 baseline.[12] Forty-five percent of the original baseline was measured again, and the remaining 55% was updated with the GDP index. Definitions were adapted: information to third parties was excluded as this is now covered in the reduction of substantive compliance costs, and business-as-usual costs (very significant) were removed. The new baseline shows EUR 9.2 billion burdens compared with EUR 16.46 billion in 2003. It should be noted that the figures are not directly comparable as the definitions have changed, and the removal of information obligations to third parties in the new baseline accounts for a major part of the difference.

- *Broader definition of compliance costs.* A new definition and methodology has been developed. The definition includes information obligations to "third parties".[13] A selection of regulations with disproportionately high-compliance costs (as identified by business) will be measured against the new definition. Thirty priority areas have been identified by working groups of officials and businesses. Seven pilot projects to test the new measurement have been completed, and have confirmed that the measurement method is practicable. The remaining pilots will shortly be completed. Concrete reduction proposals will be identified in spring 2009, and will form the basis for a percentage reduction in compliance costs in the 30 priority areas.

- *Direct interaction with business to build up the picture.* Interviews by the RRG will be used to collect information on burdens as they are experienced by business in practice, including irritants.[14] The perception monitor is a policy instrument that measures the noticeable changes in regulatory burdens, experienced by all entrepreneurs (macro level) and by individual entrepreneurs (micro level). Both levels will be monitored over a period and the changes in experience will be analysed and explained in progress reports.

- *"Fundamental surveys".* These will be based on a sector, issue, stage of a company's existence (for example start up), annoyance factor, or area of legislation. The "baseline" situation will be considered: what are the issues of public interest? What instruments (regulations, permits) are needed to safeguard these interests whilst minimising the burden?

- *Use of risk analysis* as a management tool in order to assess and reduce the risk of delays or failure of individual initiatives.

- *EU aspects.* The new baseline is split into three categories: burdens that arise entirely out of prescriptive (no room for differences) EU-origin regulations; those that arise from non-prescriptive EU-origin regulation; and those that are linked entirely to national regulations.

The zero base measurement was delivered in September 2008 in reports per ministry, along with supplements and a range of Excel tables. In addition, two calculation tools have been developed to support policy makers in their calculations and decisions on rules and regulations. The databases and tools will be used for proposals that must be submitted to ACTAL for review.

For monitoring progress, a low-tech distributed database was developed, built and implemented at the relevant ministries. A "universal fact sheet" captures all relevant facts and figures, which are registered and exchanged between the relevant ministries and the RRG. This distributed database is used for calculations on plans and results of the programme, and for reports on specific measures. Further integration with other aspects of regulation and use for communication purposes are under consideration. An "integrated review framework" is under development as part of a more comprehensive and streamlined approach to evaluation.

Public consultation and communication

A communication strategy for the programme was established by the RRG in 2007[15] drawing on recommendations of the World Bank (World Bank, 2007). This is part of the cabinet's new overall strategy for addressing regulatory burdens on business.

Despite considerable progress in the removal of unnecessary administrative burdens, the business community remained dissatisfied, and the government identified the need for better communication as one of the steps that needed to be taken to resolve the problem. The RRG Communication Plan explains that "the success of the programme will depend in part on the manner in which results are communicated to the business community. Only those companies and individual entrepreneurs who are aware of a positive change will be able to adapt their business processes accordingly and appreciate the differences in the longer term. The visibility of the changes can be enhanced by effective communication".

The RRG Communication Plan and associated handbook has an initial budget of EUR 1 million. It includes internal communication efforts to ensure that the RRG itself presents a consistent view to the outside world. It is based on one primary and several secondary target groups. The business community is the primary target, with special attention to SMEs. Different strategies have been elaborated to take account of the different sectors of the business community. The aim is to answer the question for businesses ("what is in it for me?") by presenting case studies, the challenge being to translate general results from the programme into concrete cases for the individual entrepreneur.

Secondary targets are:

- *The "intermediary" system.* This comprises sector organisations and federations, representative bodies, professional organisations, chambers of commerce, financial and legal advisers. The aim is, through these groups, to reach companies which are hard to contact directly.

- *Local authorities.* Municipalities are recognised to play an important part in reducing regulatory burdens and improving the level of service to the business community. The 31 largest municipalities and the 100 "trailblazers" are the subject of particular attention.[16] Provincial authorities and water boards are not considered so relevant at this stage.

- *The parliament, ministries and the international network.* Individual ministries are responsible for communicating their own results (as well as providing this material for RRG central communications). The handbook underlines that concrete results must have been achieved before communication, and that each message must consider what the recipient wants to know, rather than being "sender focused" as in the past (for example giving total burden reductions when the company is only interested in what it means for them).

The plan provides for a range of communication channels to capture business views directly, and to communicate results:

- One central website has been set up by the RRG to be the hub of all communications for the business community.[17] All the results of the programme are published here (including for example the regular RRG reports to the parliament). A contact point (*meldpunt regelgeving*) has also been established on the site, where businesses can submit their complaints regarding regulation (including nuisance factors). The back office is done for the RRG by *Antwoord voor Bedrijven* (answer for businesses), who pass on the issue to the relevant ministry, who must report back within four weeks on what has been done. An analysis of the results is done by the RRG as an input for their programmes. To satisfy the common commencement date principle of timely and clear provision of information, relevant websites provide companies and institutions with timely information about prospective relevant regulations.

- Regular discussions are held with representative organisations.[18]

- The compliance costs monitor and the perception monitor, which are carried out by the RRG, provide the programme with new concrete issues.

- The Minister and State Secretary of the Ministry of Economic Affairs have each "adopted" companies with the goal of better understanding the day to day problems of companies. Contacts are made twice a year.
- There are campaign with radio spots on business news radio, advertisements in business magazines, and online advertisement (banners) on other websites.
- Brochures, fact sheets on specific subjects have been produced for intermediaries such as accountants.
- Newsletters, news feeds are put on the website *www.minez.nl*.
- "Regulatory Navigators" (*branchewijzer*) provide business with information on all the regulatory obligations for their sector.

In 2008 an advertising campaign was held, with ads in magazines, brochures and radio spots, drawing attention to noticeable burden reductions. The campaign continues in 2009. The RRG have reported the following encouraging results:

- Four out of ten businesses reached.
- Two out of ten businesses remember hearing or seeing the campaign.
- Seven out of ten SMEs have absorbed the campaign message that the burden reduction programme is producing effective results, based on the fact that it helps to have better knowledge of government actions.

Achievements so far

Achievements from the 2003-07 programme[19]

The 2003-07 cabinet achieved 23% of the 25% net burden reduction target which it had set itself at the start of its term, including the following actions:

- *Annual Accounts Act* (the single most burdensome act accounting for over 15% of the total burden). Three simplification initiatives were aimed at this Act and other regulations related to accounting, including harmonising interrelated regulations, increasing thresholds and use of ICT. The total burden reduction from these initiatives was estimated at more than EUR 800 million per year.
- *Environmental regulation.* As different permits were issued by different authorities and at different levels of government, obtaining permits was time-consuming and confusing to companies. Several initiatives were aimed at reducing complexity in this area, including the single environmental permit, which replaces a number of former permits.
- *Harmonisation of wage concepts* and merger of related reports.
- *Flexibility in compliance with occupational health and safety standards,* in order to reduce burdens, by removing redundant procedures and overly formalised processes. More responsibility has been given to the social partners to take this forward.

- *Risk-oriented approach to manure legislation.* A blanket approach that applied uniformly to all farmers has been replaced with a more flexible policy.
- *Review of entire regulatory complexes.* Purple Crocodile: simplification in the wage and social security domain.

Work in progress on the 2007-11 programme

The RRG made a report to the parliament on progress with the action plan in November 2008.[20] It notes in the report that the parliament itself has a responsibility for helping to take forward the agenda, via proposals that are put to it. The report underlines that there is some way to go still. The "quick and easy" solutions no longer exist. There is a need to take EU decision-making more explicitly into account, in order to avoid a "deluge" of new regulations. The report notes that EU aspects will be given greater attention, linking the work programme to the EU regulations prioritised within the European action plan for the reduction of administrative burdens.

It also reports on work in progress to bring in the local levels of government. Pioneering local authorities are currently developing a "business effects assessment model" for summer 2008. An administrative agreement was set up in June 2007 between the central government and the local authorities. The Association of Netherlands Municipalities (VNG) is monitoring progress in achieving the local contribution to the target of 25% reduction in burdens. A baseline "zero" measurement is currently being made of local burdens, based on a sample of 25 municipalities. The baseline will be made up of two parts: burdens arising from municipalities' own regulations, and burdens linked to the implementation and enforcement of national regulations. The study was completed in June 2008 and the burdens at this level have been calculated to be EUR 125 million (100 million for the business community, 23 million for citizens and 10.5 millions "hours".

The report restates the white paper goal of achieving noticeable reductions for business. These will focus on the following areas: payroll taxes and social insurance premiums; reporting and corporate structure; environment; safety and risk management; health, youth and welfare services and child care; and service provision.

The 2007-11 work programme resets a target of 25% for the reduction of administrative burdens, which have been divided up between ministries. The total amounts to EUR 2.2 billion. Individual ministries have set out their reduction plans. As the zero base measurement shows considerable variants in the administrative burdens attached to different regulations, the reductions will not be in a "straight line" (Table 5.1).

Table 5.1. Distribution of reductions, 2007-11

	2007	2008	2009	2010	2011
min	425	789	1050	1559	2221
%	4.8	9.0	11.9	17.7	25.2

Source: Regulatory Reform Group, Dutch government.

Specific progress is reported on (among other issues) supervisory burdens and substantive compliance costs. For the former, a survey of 16 domains has now been completed, with 3 remaining. This includes the irritation caused by the working methods of inspectorates (overlap, inconsistency) and the attitude of individual inspectors (inflexible and not always sufficiently knowledgeable). The work on substantive compliance costs (see above) is also progressing.

The Netherlands Court of Audit (NCA) has carried out two evaluations of the programme, in 2006 and again in 2008. The 2006 report noted that there is an effective steering mechanism, with the cabinet behind the programme, a uniform and well-designed policy to measure burdens within a clear timeframe, but that the effects on companies have not been as anticipated. Issues linked to this included regulations that people do not comply with (the classic SCM methodology assumes 100% but it is much less); businesses have their own self-imposed burdens, which means that they will continue with a process even if it is no longer compulsory, or even reinvent a process; the cost of licences weighs especially heavily on companies. The NCA recommended that companies should have a larger input in the programme, and that the government should step up its communication on the programme. It 2008 report said it was too early to make complete comments on the (then) new action plan, but that the programme had been redirected to take more account of company views, and that there should be an expanded definition of compliance costs.

Other simplification measures for businesses

Review of business licences generated by the national level

The Ministry of Economic Affairs set up a project in 2005. An inventory of licences (defined broadly to cover as many as 20 different types of government approvals) documented the existence of approximately 1 100 different licence systems with an annual flow of 2.7 million individual licences (covering both citizens and companies). Based on a scrutiny of the inventory, the number of licence systems was reduced by 22% and the number of individual licences was reduced by 42%. This was primarily obtained by use of ICT tools (re-use of data) or by scrapping obsolete or overlapping licence systems. About 80% of this operation will be completed in 2010. A substantial part will be the result of the General Provisions (Environmental Law) Act that will combine approximately 25 licensing, exemption and other permission systems used by the Ministry of Housing, Spatial Planning and Environment and other ministries and authorities into a single environmental permit.

An example of progress put forward by the government is in the environmental field. Thirty-five thousand companies already no longer require an environmental licence. Instead they have to comply with a general set of rules. In 2010 the Environmental Licensing (General Provisions) Bill will be introduced: the new licensing system will replace much of the existing legislation regulating activities which affect the physical environment. Some 25 existing systems for issuing permits, licences, exemptions will be replaced by a single environmental licence.

The Ministry of Economic Affairs has also been working on the further introduction of *lex silencio*. All nationally generated licence systems have been reviewed by an independent agency to see if this approach was suitable. First, it was determined whether it is legally technically possible to introduce *lex silencio* (for example, no conflicting EU directives, no extensive consulting procedures with third parties). In the second step, for licence systems that passed this test, the risk to society of introducing *lex silencio* was assessed. Where *lex silencio* was possible, consideration was given to whether it was possible to abolish the permit or replace it with general rules. In December 2008 the cabinet decided that the *lex silencio* will be introduced on an extra 24 licences. A study was also commissioned to establish the existence of *lex silencio* in other countries. This study was completed in the autumn of 2008.

Review of business licences generated by municipalities

The Ministry of Economic Affairs is working with a group of local councils to determine where *lex silencio* can be applied at this level. Results in the form of a report with official recommendations will be ready in April 2009.

The Association of Netherlands Municipalities has reviewed and cut back on its model licences. Forty-six percent of the models have been abolished or simplified, which could lead to an estimated 26% reduction in burdens An estimated 70% of municipalities will introduce the new approach in 2008-09.

EU aspects

A prominent and longstanding part of the government's strategy on administrative burdens for business has been to apply pressure for action at the EU level, and encourage convergence of thinking. The 2003 baseline measurement revealed that some 40% of business burdens can be traced back to EU origin regulations. These include sizeable "complexes of administrative burdens", including VAT, company law and rules on accounting and reporting, working environment, food safety and public procurement. In 2007, ACTAL,[21] jointly with the UK Better Regulation Commission and the German *NormenKontrollRat*, submitted a series of recommendations for burden reduction to the European Commission, and a further package was sent in mid 2008.

The policy approach is four pronged:

- *Emphasis on the economic benefits for businesses, linked to the Lisbon Strategy.* Four approaches are deployed. First, political prioritisation of the EU Better Regulation Agenda (more emphasis on administrative burdens for businesses in particular) since the 2004 Dutch EU presidency. The Netherlands consider that this has encouraged the EU programme for Better Regulation to have a stronger economic character (launch of targeted EU action programme for businesses in 2006 on the basis of the Dutch methodology and approach). Second, staff secondments to the Dutch Permanent Representation and to Secretariat General, Enterprise and Internal Market, to influence developments. Third, participation in relevant networks such as the Directors of Better Regulation and its spin-off, the Standard Cost Model Network (EU co-operation and exchange of national best practices regarding the administrative burden reduction programme for businesses). Fourth, co-operation with successive EU presidencies to promote long-term planning of priorities on Better Regulation.

- *Prevention of new EU-origin administrative burdens.* This is being pursued via a stronger focus on administrative burdens in EU regulatory impact assessments (RIAs) and through targeted and active lobbying early in the EU decision-making process with like-minded member states. Additionally, systematic attention is paid to regulatory effects on businesses in the development of the national position for negotiations. Quantified estimates of expected administrative burdens for businesses arising from proposed EU legislation in the European Commission's RIA process, on the basis of the Dutch methodology, is now a requirement for European Commission RIAs.[22]

- *Tackling regulatory burdens (i.e. substantive compliance costs) in existing European regulations.* The European Commission's 2002 Action Plan for Better Regulation includes a simplification programme for existing regulation. The 2004 Dutch EU presidency organised a conference on Better Regulation and administrative burdens ("Simple is better") and co-ordinated the collection of some 300 simplification proposals from member states to feed into the programme. This work is now being used as a platform to encourage the review of substantive compliance costs in EU regulations.

- *Input for the EU Action Programme to reduce administrative burdens on business.* The Dutch government submitted a package of 55 concrete reduction proposals, which reflect the key pillars of the European Economic Recovery Plan, stressing the need to open up new finance, cut administrative burdens and kick-start investment. According to Dutch estimates these reduction proposals could lead to an additional EUR 790 million of savings to the Dutch economy and to nearly 9% of the national reduction target, if adopted by the European Commission.

The most recent initiative follows the European Commission's invitation to member states to provide input for the EU action programme to reduce administrative burdens for businesses. The Dutch Prime Minister submitted to the President of the European Commission a package of 55 concrete reduction proposals reflecting a mix of how burdens could be reduced in 14 key areas. The proposals are in line with the key pillars of the European Economic Recovery Plan, stressing the need to open up new finance, cut administrative burdens and kick-start investment. According to Dutch estimates these proposals could lead to an additional EUR 500 million savings to the Dutch economy, and to nearly 6% of the national reduction target, if adopted by the European Commission. The package covers key areas for potentially big savings, such as the working environment, public procurement, food safety, financial services, transport and accountability for government grants. It also covers high-impact proposals aimed at tackling burdens and irritants as they are experienced by businesses, particularly in areas such as statistics, agriculture, company law, environment, cohesion policy and pharmaceutical legislation.

Administrative burden reduction for citizens, professionals in the public sector and inter-governmental administrative burdens

The first programme: 2003-07

The Netherlands has a relatively longstanding policy for tackling administrative burdens on citizens. The 2003 coalition agreement extended a policy that had originally been focused exclusively on business, and added citizens as a target group for administrative burden reduction. The then government made a commitment to reduce administrative burdens for citizens by a net 25% by the end of its term of office, compared with the situation in 2002. The citizen programme was called PAL (*Programma Administratieve Lastenverlichting* – Administrative Burden Reduction Scheme for Citizens).

An early decision was to adapt the SCM methodology used for the business administrative burden reduction programme. Instead of carrying out a full-baseline measurement, the Pareto principle was used, and attention was focused on the 20% of regulations that cause 80% of the burdens. This 20% of most burdensome legislation was identified by using the list of all government services. Citizens were asked how often they used these services, and how they experienced the burdens related to these services. Eight ministries were selected for measurement and the other levels of government were also included. Only the criminal law was excluded from review. Individual ministries reviewed their own regulations, and the Ministry of Interior measured the burdens at other levels of government. Administrative burdens for citizens were expressed in hours and in out-of-pocket expenses.[23] The burden measured in this way was found, as of December 2002, to be 112 million hours annually, plus EUR 1.3 billion in out-of-pocket expenses.

The baseline measurement helped to identify important issues:

- Certain groups are particularly disadvantaged by administrative burdens. These include the chronically ill and disabled, the elderly, benefit claimants, volunteers (the "organised" citizen) and the unemployed.

- Burdens are generated by central government, provincial and local authorities, but with the main part generated by central government, which accounts for 103 million hours and nearly all out of pocket expenses. Most of the burdens from the regional and local levels can be traced back to regulations set at the national level, but for which the local and provincial levels have some discretion as to implementation.

- The most time-consuming regulation was found to be the Income Tax Act (15.1 million hours), and the most expensive regulation (generating the largest out-of-pocket expenses) was the Netherlands Civil Code (EUR 745 million). The Civil Code regulates *inter alia* the establishment of mortgages by notarial deed and conveyance. The Road Traffic Act also scored highly, both in terms of time and expenses, as it imposes an annually recurring burden on a large number of citizens.

First results were reported in a May 2006 report, which indicated that a net reduction of EUR 25.7 million hours and EUR 326 million costs would be achieved by the end of 2007, meaning that the 25% would have been met by that date, both in terms of time and of costs. Due to the fall of the cabinet in November 2006 the target was not met by the end of 2007. However, the target will be met at the end of 2011.

Current policy: Action Plan for the Top Ten Bottlenecks, and Life Analysis

After the 2006 elections the new cabinet decided to continue the programme but in a different way, with more emphasis on a qualitative approach, via the identification of the "top ten" most irritating burdens for citizens and the development of "life analysis". There is no new baseline measurement and a quantified reduction target is no longer promoted. Experience in the first phase of the programme had led to the conclusion that it was important for reduction measures to be noticed by citizens, but that this was a major challenge.[24] Research commissioned by the Ministry of Interior noted that: "Although the results (so far) appear to be favourable, citizens don't seem to notice a lot of it yet… which raises the question whether the current efforts have the desired effect".

The research looked "bottom up" at how citizens experienced their interaction with bureaucracy, found that the experiences were intensely individualistic and that citizens wanted freedom to manage their situation in a context (for some) of intense dependence on government.[25] The research came up with a roadmap concept, as well as a redefinition of was meant by an administrative burden, and five steps to a noticeable reduction. The five steps were to describe the purpose (of the service); determine the position within the relation model (how do/will citizens perceive the service from their perception of freedom?); read out protocol and character (how does the service fit within the relationship between government and citizen); compare or design (assess the extent to which the current service design fits the relationship between government and citizen); take measures (to align the service to the desired approach).

The new approach applies four main methods to reduce burdens:[26]

- simplification or removal of rules or procedures;
- use of ICT;
- common information infrastructure for public service providers, so that data is only provided once (data re-use); and
- general rules or frameworks, to replace licences and permits.

Top ten bottlenecks

The "top ten bottlenecks" which matter most to citizens were identified as:

- *Quick and reliable.* The goal is to assess waiting/processing times for government and municipal services, and to shorten these, not least (but not only) with the support of Internet. The emphasis is also on transparency, giving citizens the opportunity to check on the status of their application (for a building permit for example), as well as publishing overall data on processing times.
- *Simple application and justification of social security benefits.* The goal is simple electronic applications and more efficient justification of significant social security benefits. This is especially aimed at vulnerable people who face a lot of paperwork and engage with many different arms of government to claim benefits. Single integrated contact and processing points are being developed.
- *Submitting personal details only once.* The goal is to provide access to all income related regulations on one internet page.
- *Getting a travel document easily.* The goal is to enable citizens to apply for passports and ID cards at any town hall. An online travel document database will be created (this requires a change in the law).
- *Fewer permits, towards general rules.* The goal is to avoid delays by simplifying the current system of numerous individual permits, through simplification and a reduction in the number of permits, as well as access to permit information on line. The number of permits can be reduced by using general rules. Among other issues this involves the municipalities in a fundamental review of their model regulations.
- *User friendly forms.* The goal is simplified forms for change of address notifications, requests for services, etc. Incomprehensible forms are high on the list of bottlenecks.
- *More trust.* The goal is to trust people more, for example, by introducing more subsidies within health and social services that do not need to be justified.
- *Lending an ear.* The goal is to solve problems with the authorities through *ex ante* mediation, rather than legally through complaint procedures. Research shows that this results in reduced costs for the organisation and more satisfied customers and officials.

- *Give volunteers more freedom.* The goal is to treat volunteer organisations as groups of individuals instead of as a business, so that their work is less complicated. Currently they are treated as businesses.

- *Quality comes first.* The goal is a rating of at least seven out of ten for the quality of government services. A methodology has been developed to measure quality.

Life analysis

Nine life analyses were developed with "roadmaps" to show the routes that citizens had to take through the bureaucracy, from their viewpoint (benefit claimant, volunteer, disabled child, senile older person, average family, healthy older person, chronically ill, pensioner, unemployed). Three areas stood out with the highest burdens: tax declarations, obtaining/renewing a passport, and obtaining/renewing a driving licence.

Institutional framework

The programme is led by the Ministry of Interior, with a state secretary in charge and a project team (REAL: Programme Regulatory and Administrative Burdens) of around 18 staff, working in three clusters (national/international, municipalities and public sector). One contact point in the Ministry of Interior has been established for each of the ten bottlenecks. Each ministry has a nominated co-ordinator. Ministries are responsible for developing their own action plan to address the burdens. There is a standard reporting template on progress. An inter-ministerial group of officials (ICRAL – Interdepartmental Commission of Co-ordinators for the Reduction of Administrative Burdens for Citizens) provides support and networking between ministries.

ACTAL plays an important challenge role. All new government proposals with possible effects on administrative burdens on citizens or businesses must be sent to ACTAL for advice, before they can be sent to the cabinet. The advice is not binding, but weighs in the final decision as ministries can and do use it in evidence. ACTAL is also empowered to advise on existing burdens.

Municipalities are formally engaged in the programme, via a June 2007 High-Level Governing Board Agreement, and the follow up Implementation Schedule of October 2007 (which bring together VNG, and the Interior, Finance and Economic Affairs ministries). A task force of officials operates at local level, linked to "pioneer" municipalities which have agreed to develop best practice that could be adopted by others. Since April 2009 a group of regional "ambassadors" (mayors and aldermen) has been established. These ambassadors will stimulate local governments in their region to use the instruments and best practices on reducing burdens already developed by the Ministry of Interior and to (local) authorities. The Ministry of Interior supports municipalities financially to help them meet the 25% target on administrative burdens for citizens at local level, which includes the VNG's work to simplify model regulations. There is a quality of service improvement target for this level, and an emphasis on comprehensible forms, as well as a review of model regulations. Some of this work is linked to implementation of the EU Services Directive.

Annual reports are made by the Ministry of Interior to the Ministerial Steering Group for Better Regulation chaired by the Prime Minister. There is also a progress report to the parliament once a year (the Ministry of Interior's report on e-Government is integrated in this report).

Use of e-Government

ICT is one of the main tools for the programme, and the Ministry of Interior estimates that 40% of burden reductions for citizens are ICT related. The aim is not just process reengineering, but a change in the underlying regulations where appropriate. The ICT structure (which is partly shared with the business programme) is being developed on the basis of a number of "building blocks:

- *Electronic access. Mijnoverheid.nl* (*mygovernemnt.nl*) personalised two-way Internet exchanges for information and services with the government via Internet. *Antwoord* for citizens and *Antwoord voor Bedrijven* (answer for enterprises): telephone based one-stop shops at municipality level.

- *E-authentication.* DigiD: Electronic authentication code for access to government electronic services such as tax declaration). Six million people already use DigiD.

- *Single government number. Burger Service Nummer* (Citizens Service Number): The government aims to use a single number in its contacts with citizens, businesses and other government organisations.

- *Key registers.* The aim is to have one key register of information on citizens by 2010, so that the latter only have to supply it once.

Consultation and communication

Significant efforts have been made to communicate and discuss the programme, both internally and to external stakeholders, including specific citizen target groups. Communication tools are varied. They include brochures, websites, instruction manuals, newsletters, articles in national newspapers, seminars, workshops, meetings, conferences and material for television programmes. Citizens' panels are regularly convened, and there is a specific monitor on municipalities to show developments in service delivery. The approach is adapted as needs arise or the need for extra effort is identified.

The "*Kafkabrigade*" initiative is based around a group of experts who seek to solve problems in the public sector from the perspective of citizens. There is a brief investigation into a specific problem and how it is handled by the government. Civil servants are involved in this process. An appraisal review is then carried with the authorities involved, as a result of which the *Kafkabrigade* formulates recommendations for improving the way the system works.

A "*Museum of Needless Policies*" has also been established. This is a travelling exhibition on which citizens (and the authorities) can exhibit their examples of needless policies. Any level of government can host the museum, on condition that it provides one example of its own needless policy accompanied with a piece of art. The museum seeks to foster a change of attitude toward regulations, and may spark discussions on specific regulations.

A key part of the communication policy is via the Internet. A hyperlink to the website "burdened by government[27] has been placed on the websites of more than 100 municipalities. The website offers citizens an accessible means of lodging their comments and complaints. Similar websites have been developed for inter-governmental burdens[28] and burdens for professionals in the public sector.[29]

The programme seeks to consult directly with citizens and their representative groups, including citizens' panels, on the development of the programme. The ten bottlenecks were identified and are being addressed in dialogue with these groups, which will also be asked to report on whether an obstacle has been resolved.

EU aspects

The Ministry of Interior has been active in encouraging the European Commission to take an interest in administrative burdens on citizens.[30] The state secretary responsible for the programme sent a letter to the European Commission in January 2008 drawing attention to some of the problems that could be directly traced to EU-origin regulations. The letter notes that 23% of administrative burdens on citizens in the Netherlands in time, and 15% in costs, have their origin at EU level, and cites several examples, including the costs.[31] The letter also underlines the need for the European Commission's impact assessment system to assess and quantify social impacts more clearly, so that new EU regulation does not increase burdens. It adds that there is also a responsibility on member states to reduce burdens and that the Netherlands has established an informal European network to help this along. In addition, the Ministry of Interior initiated a common reaction on the EU consultation on the impact assessment guidelines, which called for a quantitative measurement of the administrative burdens for citizens in the impact assessment guidelines. This common reaction was submitted in co-operation with seven other European countries. In 2008 the Ministry of Interior established a "Learning Team on Administrative Burdens for Citizens" within the EUPAN framework. By the end of 2008 more than 20 European countries were participating in the Learning Team."What a Relief" is the website that has been set up to exchange knowledge and experience in the field of administrative burden reduction for citizens between European countries that are members of this Learning Team.[32] Finally, it has also developed three profiles of "mobile European citizens" on which to map their burdens, with a view to proposing practical reduction measures which could be used for benchmarking across Europe.

Administrative burden reduction inside the administration

A part of the citizen programme addresses regulation inside the administration, notably for professionals working in public services such as hospitals and schools. The aim is to free up time spent on administration so that more time can be spent on their "real jobs" and services to citizens enhanced. There are three full-time equivalent staff on this work. The Ministry of Interior report to the parliament notes that the burdens of professionals in the public sector should be reduced substantially. Specific objectives include reducing the amount of information that must be recorded, developing a single audit, standardising definitions, and streamlining the benefit system. "Registration requirements" for teachers and police will be cut back. Profiles of professionals (akin to the citizen profiles already created) have been developed. In co-operation with the professionals themselves a top five of administrative burdens per profile will be selected. The programme will work on solving these burdens. There will be surveys to check progress. Committees have been established with other ministries and professional bodies to monitor and advise on progress. Another part of the programme addresses burdens between levels of government, more specifically the burdens between central government and the local level of government. Specific objectives here include reducing the amount of information that must be recorded, developing a single audit, standardising definitions, downsizing the number of ring-fenced special purpose grants to local government and streamlining the benefit system. The project aims to reduce inter-governmental burdens by 25%.

Notes

1. Programmes to reduce administrative burdens may include the review and simplification of whole regulatory frameworks or laws, so there can be some overlap with policies aimed at simplification via consolidation, etc. There may also be some overlap with the previous chapter on the development of new regulations, as administrative burden reduction programmes are often conducted on a net basis, that is, taking account of the impact of new regulations in meeting target reductions.

2. Simplification can take different technical forms. The 2001 EU *Mandelkern* report identified several definitions which are now used by the EU institutions. Recasting brings together multiple texts that regulate a particular area into one, with or without minor changes to the substance, producing a text without legal effect but of practical benefit. Consolidation means bringing together multiple texts that regulate a particular area into one, with or without minor changes to the substance, producing a text without legal effect but of practical benefit. Codification means consolidating all the amendments made over time to a given law, which are often implemented through additional laws. Within the EU Institutions, the specific definition is repealing a set of acts in one area and replacing them with a single act containing no substantive change to those acts, thus producing a text with legal effect.

3. To note that the Netherlands programme is now called the "Regulatory Burden Reduction Programme", reflecting a move beyond administrative burdens and towards broader compliance costs.

4. The 2007 World Bank Group report "Review of the Dutch Administrative Burden Reduction Programme" noted calculations by Kox (2005) suggesting that the 25% reduction in the Netherlands will reduce administrative burdens from 3.7% of GDP to 2.8% of GDP, which is significantly above the United Kingdom (1.5%) and Denmark (1.9%). (World Bank, 2007).

5. One example given to the team was a proposal to simplify regular technical controls on cars. It was originally planned to reduce the frequency of such controls from one to every two years. Pressure from garage owners meant an adaptation of the proposal to cover only petrol vehicles.

6. The OECD team were told, and this is not specific to the Netherlands, that business finds it hard to understand why takes so long to change a regulation. Management of expectations is important.

7. The OECD team were told that behaviour at the local level had not yet noticeably changed.

8. See Annex B for a fuller description of the programme's evolution over time.

9. *Meet Instument Administratieve Lastendruk.*

10. Silence is consent.

11. They must report twice a year, linked to their budget reporting cycle, including a statement of expected increases and reductions respectively over the four-year cabinet period, and explain deviations from previous reports.

12. The original baseline measurement cost about EUR 3 million, including the development of the methodology. To these external costs should be added the cost of staffing. IPAL (the RRG's predecessor) had about 18 full-time employees and

ACTAL 12 teams (2-4 persons, who often also worked on related Better Regulation issues such as licence simplification) also worked on the measurement in each ministry. The baseline update involved 100 consultants, 44 days work and cost EUR 4.5 million, excluding ministry resources.

13. These costs were formerly considered to be administrative burdens, but cannot be accounted for as information obligations from the government, as they cover information exchange between civil parties (even though they are obligatory, *e.g.* insurance companies that deal with health insurance are obliged to report yearly to their customers about their "consumption of healthcare".) They have therefore been redefined as compliance costs.

14. Irritants can be perverse. One especially striking example given to the team was the recycling of water for power plants to the river. This may raise the quality of the water, which then has to be reduced in order to meet a fixed quality norm. Another example given was the need for frequent measurement of puddles beside public swimming pools to check for pollution.

15. Regulatory Reform Group, "Action Plan Red Tape Reduction for Businesses in the Netherlands 2007-11, Communication Plan".

16. Local authorities that have agreed to take part in various trial projects, following a 2006 initiative by the Ministry of Economic Affairs.

17. *www.antwoordvoorbedrijven.nl* (answer for businesses).

18. For example, *VNO-NCW, MKB-Nederland.*

19. For further background, see the 2007 OECD/World Bank report.

20. One of the four regular reports that it is required to make every year, two major ones, and two shorter updates.

21. Together with its British and German counterparts.

22. More recently the Netherlands contributed to the public consultation on the European Commission's revised RIA guidelines. One of its key regulatory standpoints was that the usefulness of impact assessments as an operational instrument for European political decision making can be increased by a cover note stating the main outcomes, such as expected costs and benefits of the various options and the corresponding net effects on businesses.

23. For example, the cost of a notary to buy a house, public transport tickets, phone calls.

24. The Ministry of Interior did say to the OECD peer review team that public perceptions were of a significant improvement in waiting times, although there were still black spots.

25. "Five steps to a noticeable administrative burden reduction", November 2006. This was followed by a novel approach: the ministry commissioned research from an industrial design bureau more accustomed to develop visions for the corporate sector that could be translated into products or services.

26. Government document on the Action Plan, January 2007.

27. *www.lastvandeoverheid.nl* (burdened by the government).

28. *www.interbestuurlijkelasten.nl.*

29. *www.mijnechtewerk.nl.*

30. The Ministry of Interior report to the parliament in September 2007 noted that some 20% of administrative burdens for citizens may be linked to EU- origin regulations.

31. One example is the Energy Performance Building Directive 2002/91/EG. This is estimated to lead to an increase in burdens for Dutch citizens of 95 000 hours and EUR 28 million p.a.

32. *www.whatarelief.eu.*

Chapter 6

Compliance, enforcement, appeals

Whilst adoption and communication of a law sets the framework for achieving a policy objective, effective implementation, compliance and enforcement are essential for actually meeting the objective. An *ex ante* assessment of compliance and enforcement prospects is increasingly a part of the regulatory process in OECD countries. Within the EU's institutional context these processes include the correct transposition of EU rules into national legislation (this aspect will be considered in Chapter 7).

The issue of proportionality in enforcement, linked to risk assessment, is attracting growing attention. The aim is to ensure that resources for enforcement should be proportionately higher for those activities, actions or entities where the risks of regulatory failure are more damaging to society and the economy (and conversely, proportionately lower in situations assessed as lower risk).

Rule-makers must apply and enforce regulations systematically and fairly, and regulated citizens and businesses need access to administrative and judicial review procedures for raising issues related to the rules that bind them, as well as timely decisions on their appeals. Tools that may be deployed include administrative procedures acts, the use of independent and standardised appeals processes,[1] and the adoption of rules to promote responsiveness, such as "silence is consent".[2] Access to review procedures ensures that rule-makers are held accountable.

Review by the judiciary of administrative decisions can also be an important instrument of quality control. For example scrutiny by the judiciary may capture whether subordinate rules are consistent with the primary laws, and may help to assess whether rules are proportional to their objective.

Assessment and recommendations

The Netherlands has engaged in pioneer work to ensure that compliance and enforcement are considered at the start of the rule-making process. This was already picked up in the OECD's 1999 report but deserves to be repeated, in the context of today's interest across the OECD in tackling policy related to the enforcement of regulations as well as their development. Efforts by the Ministry of Justice to raise awareness go back over two decades, via the Directives on Legislation (which it drafts), the legal quality criteria which it applies, and the Practicability and Enforcement Impact Assessment which it also applies. The Netherlands is also responsible for the development of the so called "*Table of Eleven*" determinants of compliance, which have widely influenced other countries' efforts in this field.

There has also been steady development toward a new risk-based approach and structures for enforcement. A well-articulated policy which engages the local as well as national levels has been refined through successive cabinets, starting in 2001. Local levels are formally engaged through the central government agreement with municipalities, including pilots for new approaches with a sample of pioneer municipalities.

Recommendation 6.1. The government should consider how it can share experiences and ideas on more effective enforcement with other countries, both to learn from them and to disseminate its own successes.

The establishment of the co-ordinating Inspection Council to promote the new approach has been a successful move and there is close co-operation with the work of the RRG. Is the Ministry of Justice fully engaged? The council came across to the OECD peer review team as motivated and enthusiastic in its role. There is a close link with the regulatory burden reduction programme for business (reflected in the fact that a reduction of state supervision forms part of the current action plan for the reduction of administrative burdens on business) and close involvement by the RRG in this work. The involvement of the Ministry of Justice, which has played a longstanding upstream role in drawing attention to compliance and enforcement when regulations are developed, is not so clear. Yet the reform programme implies the need to address regulations as they are developed, as much as how they are implemented once adopted.

Recommendation 6.2. The Ministry of Justice needs to be fully engaged in developing the programme, especially as the current Framework Vision seeks to promote a fundamental reform of attitudes to underlying rules and policy.

The current Framework Vision is ambitious as well as quite precise in its goals: careful evaluation of progress is essential if credibility and momentum are to be sustained. The results to date set out in the 2008 report to the parliament appear to be impressive. The report documents for example the establishment of joint risk analyses between inspectorates, co-operation between inspectorates and municipalities, facilities for digital co-operation, and the reassignment of tasks. What has been the real effect of these reforms on the ground? Are these the right targets?

Recommendation 6.3. Steps should be taken to ensure that regular and independent evaluations are carried of the results emerging from the Framework Vision.

The research report of the Ministry of Justice on the state of compliance is a useful initiative to back up further reform. The results should be directly relevant to the further development of the Framework Vision.

Background

Compliance and enforcement

An early start to embed compliance and enforcement in regulatory policy

The Netherlands was a pioneer among OECD countries in seeking to address issues of compliance and enforcement as part of the process of making regulations. The Directives on Legislation, which go back to 1972, and the Ministry of Justice framework for securing legal quality before a proposal can be submitted to cabinet for approval (see Chapter 4) require regulators to ensure, before adopting a regulation, that they will be able to "adequately" enforce it. The directives require rule makers to consider explicitly whether enforcement under administrative, civil or criminal law would be most appropriate. Explanatory notes specify general legislative drafting principles for improving enforceability, including minimising scope for different interpretations, minimising exceptions, directing rules at "situations which are visible or which can be objectively established" and ensuring practicability for both enforcers and the regulated. One of the six criteria which make up the legal quality framework explicitly addresses feasibility and enforceability. To further underline that compliance and enforcement needs early attention in the rule-making process, a "Practicability and Enforcement Assessment" (P&E) is part of the current Dutch impact assessment process. This facilitates identification of the effects of proposed legislation for implementing and enforcement authorities, including ministries, agencies, but also authorities such as the police, Public Prosecutor's Office and judiciary.

Table of Eleven

A further important and longstanding dimension is the Inspectorate of Law, now called the Expert Centre on the Administration of Justice and Law Enforcement, within the Ministry of Justice, which acts as consultant to ministries on issues of enforcement in relation to regulatory proposals. The Expert Centre regards enforceability assessment as essentially probabilistic, recognising that there is significant uncertainty. It aims to identify the two or three key "risk factors" for compliance/enforcement in relation to each regulatory proposal to enable policy makers to address these issues in advance. The review is made as consistent as possible through adoption of standard checklists and other instruments. A key tool is the "Table of Eleven" determinants of compliance.[3]

Box 6.1. The Table of Eleven

This was developed jointly by the Ministry of Justice and Erasmus University and derives from academic literature in the areas of social psychology, sociology and criminology, supplemented by the Ministry's practical experiences and viewpoints on law enforcement. The table is in three parts:

- *Spontaneous compliance dimensions.* These are factors that affect the incidence of voluntary compliance - that is, compliance which would occur in the absence of enforcement. They include the level of knowledge and understanding of the rules, the benefits and costs of complying, the level of acceptance of the "reasonableness" of the regulations, general attitudes to compliance by the target group and "informal control", and the possibility of non-compliance being sanctioned by non- government actors.

- *Control dimensions.* This group of factors determines the probability of detection of non-complying behaviour. The probability of detection is directly related to the level of compliance. The factors considered are the probability of third parties revealing non-compliance, the probability of inspection by government officials, the probability of inspection actually uncovering non-compliance and the ability of inspection authorities to target inspections effectively.

- *Sanctions dimensions.* The third group of factors determines the expected value of sanctions for non-compliance, that is, the probability of a sanction being imposed where non-compliance is detected and the severity and type of likely sanctions.

Development of a risk-based approach to enforcement

Reforms have been ongoing for a number of years, as part of the process of modernising central government, under parliamentary pressure for change, and because of pressures generated by civil service reforms and staff cuts. Inspectorates and other enforcement agencies in the Netherlands now commonly use a risk-based approach to enforcement, carrying out risk analysis based on estimations or measurement of non-compliance and the maximum credible effect of non-compliance, tailored to the sector in question. Risks are prioritised in discussion with parent ministries.

First reform steps: The 2001 and 2005 Framework Visions on Inspection and Supervision

The fireworks disaster in 2000 in Enschede drew sharp attention to the issue of inspection and enforcement in the Netherlands. This led in 2001 to the first Framework Vision on Inspection and Supervision. The first vision was broadened and developed in 2005 into a second Framework Vision. The second vision was taken forward through various initiatives which continued until the end of 2007.

Current policy: The ambition for 2010 and the Inspection Simplification Programme

The current cabinet has endorsed the continuation of a Framework Vision, setting out its vision for 2010 in a letter to the parliament. It also follows up on another parliamentary motion.[4] The objective is to continue the modernisation of central government inspection so that it promotes trust, takes firm action where required, provides better services, operates in close co-operation with other inspectorates at central and local government level, and interacts effectively with government policy and lawmaking. The government wants to reduce the number of government bodies involved, and apply advanced methods with a smaller organisation. The vision in terms of how companies, institutions and professionals are to experience inspections by 2010 is described thus

Box 6.2. Inspections: The Ambition

"Inspectors act on the assumption that we want to adhere to the rules. Business operations involving major hazards are monitored more intensively than they used to be and processes which carry less risk are monitored less frequently. Methods of inspection have also changed. The inspectorates make maximum use of our quality systems and our data. If these are satisfactory the inspectorate will focus mainly on checking the system. National inspectorates and municipalities etc. all collaborate well, which means we are approached by fewer inspectorates and no longer have to answer the same questions twice. The inspectors are skilled and are receptive to our operational processes. They communicate clearly about their tasks and the results. Rules have become less complex and are fewer in number. Observing them entails no disproportionate effort. Inspectors communicate clearly which rules apply to us, their nature and how we should incorporate them. If the rules are deliberately ignored, inspectors act quickly and firmly".

Source: Letter from the Dutch Minister of the Interior and Kingdom Relations to the parliament, January 2008.

This ambition rests on four pillars. The first two elements are the continuation and intensification of existing initiatives and mainly concern the central government inspectorates. The remaining two promote a more fundamental reform with their focus on the underlying rules, policy, and societal concepts that underpin the role of the inspectorates:

- *Modernisation and quality (streamlining structures, collaboration and modern risk-based approaches).* Inspection and supervision will be reorganised into domains and/or chains, recognisable for the stakeholder, with a single front office for each domain, and relevant inspectorates collaborating in the back office. Cross-government analyses drawn up by the inspectorates will provide insight into the main risks in the defined domains. ICT will be deployed to facilitate exchange of information between inspectorates. Promotion of a cultural shift under which inspectors will trust that stakeholders are willing to comply, act proportionately, communicate clearly, and offer advice, with peer assessment to make this stick. Inspectors will make as much use as possible of control systems such as quality assurance systems for companies (certification and accreditation) which minimise burdens. The work is to be based on "lenient where possible, strict where required". The Netherlands notes that the international dimension limits modernisation, EU approaches not always being well adapted to a more flexible system because of an emphasis on regulatory harmonisation and the need to develop a level playing field within the EU. Inspectorates (and parent ministries) are therefore encouraged to play a proactive role internationally in support of more flexible methods.

- *Transferred tasks and clustered expertise (more efficient reorganisation of tasks).* Where necessary tasks will be transferred between central government inspectorates (and hence ministries). Grouping will be carried out where possible according to sector (*e.g.* SMEs, child services), for joint inspections (including "joint regulations" for integrated enforcement) as well establishment of lead inspectorates with authority to act on behalf of others. This is already happening with the Labour Inspectorate, Housing, Spatial Planning and the Environment Inspectorate. Tasks will be allocated according to "operational scale", with a related reassignment of tasks between inspectorates. Central government inspectorates may operate on behalf of other layers of government. Some routine tasks may be privatised.

- *Regulations and policy (more flexible regulatory approach).* This is the Inspection Reform Programme. It consists of a review of existing regulations to determine whether alternative instruments could be used. Where possible, regulations will be linked to target standards (check lists, performance indicators) rather than specific provisions (in short, giving inspectors more flexibility).

- *Government accountability (promoting a new understanding of the limits of government responsibility in risk management).* The focus is on managing public and political concepts of the role of inspectorates, given often conflicting views on risk and the public interest. "Society will need to accept that government cannot be responsible for protection against all risks. Adequate attention must be paid to this policy."

The Inspection Reform Programme

To give effect to the Framework Visions, an Inspection Reform Programme (which used to be known as the Inspection Simplification Programme) has been set up by each ministry across its area of responsibility.

Box 6.3. Main results to date of the Inspection Simplification Programme

- Burden measurements have been concluded in 16 domains and are ongoing in 3 others;
- A maximum of two standard government inspections each year for SMEs is now in place in four domains, is scheduled for two domains, and was already in place in seven others;
- Front offices have been set up in ten domains, are in preparation in eight others;
- Approach and attitude: incorporation of a fresh approach and attitude in six domains; attunement between existing inspectorate training programmes;
- Co-operation between inspectorates: joint annual plans achieved in nine domains and in preparation in nine others; risk analyses drawn up in four domains, scheduled in ten others;
- Co-operation with other regulators: 50 municipalities, 8 provinces and 4 water authorities involved in current or scheduled pilots in 17 domains;
- Transfer of tasks: in six domains various monitoring tasks have been reassigned between central government inspectorates; transfer of tasks is under scrutiny in nine domains; privatisation of inspection tasks in the agricultural and horticultural sectors;
- ICT: eight facilities for digital co-operation have been developed and tested, partly in co-operation with municipalities; and
- Boundary framework for information exchange: legal requirements have been considered and translated into practical guidelines; covenants between inspectorates are being prepared.

Source: Letter from the Dutch Minister of the Interior and Kingdom Relations to the parliament, January 2008

Institutional framework

The strategy engages four lead ministries: the Ministry of Interior (general responsibility for inspection and supervision, as well as a co-ordination role for local levels of government), the Ministry of Economic Affairs and the Ministry of Finance (regulatory burden reduction programme for business) and the Ministry of Justice (legal quality and law enforcement, as well as general legal hurdles that need attention such as the privacy laws from extending the use of ICT such as data exchange).

The practical roll out of the programme is overseen by the Inspection Council, made up of the heads of the 14 state inspectorates.[5] The council is a vehicle for collaboration and for the further professionalisation of inspection activities in accordance with the Framework Visions, and for specific programmes concerning state inspection.[6] Advisory members represent the Ministry of Interior and the Ministry of Justice. The council's bureau has a budget of EUR 2.5 million for 2009, funded by the inspectorates. For building and implementing joint ICT applications, the programme was granted a EUR 24.5 million budget by the Central Government Reform Programme, topped up by inspectorates by the same amount. The council, assisted by a small bureau, co-ordinates much of the Inspection Simplification Programme (apart from policy-related issues such as the review of regulations, which is done by the parent ministries). The secretaries of state of the four lead ministries jointly monitor the programme. The Ministry of Interior and Kingdom Relations monitors the programme. The Prime Minister's Steering Group for Better Regulation intervenes as necessary. There are regular progress reports to the parliament, including the Inspection Council's annual report.

Responsibility for enforcement on the ground is shared by national inspectorates and municipalities.

There are fourteen national inspectorates (*inspecties*). They have their own executive and budget. These inspectorates are set up according to a limited number of templates as regards budget and legal arrangements, although their tasks and responsibilities vary. Parent ministries are ultimately accountable for their work and decisions.[7]

Local government dimension

The Central Government Agreement with the Municipalities (see Chapter 8) connects them with the general policy for enforcement reform and the development of a more risk-based approach. The central inspectorates have co-ordinated with local government to map the situation and have found that some of the most important issues arise at the local level. To make progress, an adapted version of the SCM methodology has been used, including irritants. Specific areas are examined to establish what matters most for the recipient of enforcement activity.[8] Pilot programmes have been established with some municipalities and provinces.

Research project on compliance

The research institute of the Ministry of Justice is currently examining the general level of compliance in a project called "The state of compliance". The project is expected to be completed in 2009 and is considering:

- *The state of compliance.* In what respect is compliance measured or estimated? What perspectives, methods and techniques are used? What kind of information is available and what sectors and target policy groups does it cover?

- *What kind of information results from current compliance?* To what extent do target groups comply with the law? What's the cause and character of non-compliance? What kind of differences and similarities can be found in non-compliance within certain target groups or policy areas?

Appeals

The General Administrative Act contains procedures for appeal against administrative decisions, including those relating to regulatory enforcement. Administrative appeals are heard by the administrative branch of the courts, and in appeal by specific administrative courts.[9] Appeals are always preceded by an objection procedure (*bezwaar*) with the body that took the initial decision. It is usual for these cases to be heard by a single-judge division, but the district court can decide to appoint three judges to a case which is complex or which involves fundamental issues. In cases involving civil servants and social security issues, appeal is a matter for a special tribunal, the Central Appeals Tribunal, and in most other cases for the Administrative Jurisdiction Division of the Council of State.[10]

Notes

1. Administrative review by the regulatory enforcement body, administrative review by an independent body, judicial review, ombudsman.

2. Some of these aspects are covered elsewhere in the report.

3. *www.justitie.nl/onderwerpen/opsporing%5Fen%5Fhandhaving/rechtshandhaving/producten%5Finstrumenten%5Fmethodes/T11.*

4. Submitted by Brigitte van der Burg MP.

5. General Inspection Service for Agriculture, Nature and Food Quality, Labour Inspectorate, Health Care Inspectorate, Inspectorate for Public Order and Safety, Inspectorate of Transport, Public Works and Water Management, Education Inspectorate, State Inspectorate for Cultural Heritage, Food and Consumer Product Safety Authority, Inspectorate of Housing, Spatial Planning and the Environment. There are other types of agency under this category, such as the State Archive Agency.

6. A parliamentary motion submitted by Charlie Aptroot MP proposing a merger of inspectorates led to its establishment as well as to the Inspection Simplification Programme.

7. The agricultural sector was measured for example- what did farmers think? It found that they didn't mind lots of inspections, provided that they were short and didn't coincide with farming's busiest periods. Entrepreneurs in other sectors do mind lots of inspections, particularly if the same questions are asked more than once. Irritants in regard to inspectors are lack of knowledge, mistrusting attitude and lack of feedback.

8. General Inspection Service for Agriculture, Nature and Food Quality, Labour Inspectorate, Health Care Inspectorate, Inspectorate for Public Order and Safety, Inspectorate of Transport, Public Works and Water Management, Education Inspectorate, State Inspectorate for Cultural Heritage, Food and Consumer Product Safety Authority, Inspectorate of Housing, Spatial Planning and the Environment. There are other types of agency under this category, such as the State Archive Agency.

9. The Council of State (for cases relating to the environment, spatial planning, immigration), the Centrale Raad van Beroep (for cases relating to the Civil Service Act – *Ambtenarenwet*) and the College *van Beroep voor het Bedrijfsleven* (for cases relating to agriculture and other economic sectors).

10. Generally speaking, appeals against judgements of courts of first instance in administrative matters can be lodged with the Council of State.) For specific categories other courts of appeal are competent: the *Centrale Raad van Beroep* (for cases relating to the Civil Service Act – *Ambtenarenwet*) and the *College van Beroep voor het Bedrijfsleven* (for cases relating to agriculture and other economic sectors).

Chapter 7

The interface between member states and the European Union

An increasing proportion of national regulations in EU member states originate at EU level. Whilst EU regulations[1] have direct application in member states and do not have to be transposed into national regulations, EC directives need to be transposed, raising the issue of how to ensure that the regulations implementing EC law are fully coherent with the underlying policy objectives, do not create new barriers to the smooth functioning of the EU Single Market, avoid "gold plating" and the placing of unnecessary burdens on business and citizens. Transposition also needs to be timely, to minimise the risk of uncertainty as regards the state of the law, especially for business.

The national (and subnational) perspective on how the production of regulations is managed in Brussels itself is important. Better Regulation policies, including impact assessment, have been put in place by the European Commission to improve the quality of EU law. The view from "below" on the effectiveness of these policies may be a valuable input to improving them.

Assessment and recommendations

Consciousness of the importance of EU-origin regulations in shaping the national regulatory environment is high, and the Netherlands are active participants in the development of EU-level Better Regulation strategies. For a relatively small country, the Netherlands have been commendably active in raising consciousness of Better Regulation principles at EU level, so that problems are tackled at source, including most recently the importance of effective EU management to keep down burdens on citizens.[2]

Well-structured processes are in place for the negotiation and transposition of EU regulations. As in most other EU countries, the Netherlands have developed and established a clear procedural framework for dealing with EU regulations. A particularly strong feature is the process for establishing an implementation plan when an EU regulation is adopted, in which the local levels of government are invited to participate, and the subsequent monitoring of transposition via a centrally co-ordinated database (run by the Ministry of Justice) which systematically tracks and disseminates progress in meeting deadlines for implementation. Transparency as regards the correlation between EU and national regulations is covered under the framework. The processes for ensuring consistency between EU and national regulations (which extend to taking account of the rulings of the European courts) are also noteworthy.

The framework is more effective in securing a sound procedural performance than in addressing issues of substance arising from EU regulations. The EU was a recurring theme across the interviews with the OECD peer review team, with concerns expressed by a number of stakeholders inside and outside government at the difficulties of managing the process of rule-making at this level and implementation into the national context. These included a concern about staying up to date with EU developments, with information sometimes being available too late to affect the outcome, and about failures to pay sufficient attention to likely national impacts of EU regulations both at the negotiation and transposition phase of the process. For example the packaging directive was gold plated in transposition. Although the local levels have a formal seat at the committee tables to discuss these matters, the team also heard that more targeted efforts should be made to involve these levels where needed. The most fundamental critique of the current approach was the failure to assess impacts adequately. There is currently no requirement for impact assessment at the negotiation phase, and it is not clear how much is actually done at the transposition phase. The Ministry of Foreign Affairs and the Ministry of Justice lead the various processes, which may leave the framework short of input from other key Better Regulation ministries (Interior, Finance and Economic Affairs).

Recommendation 7.1. The government should carry out a review of current processes for the negotiation and transposition of EU regulations, in order to map strengths and weaknesses, to deepen the involvement of the Interior, Finance and Economic Affairs ministries, and to strengthen procedures and guidance aimed at addressing substantive issues. Impact assessment of EU regulations both at the negotiation and transposition phase should be made a formal requirement and an integral part of the new impact assessment process as proposed in Chapter 4.

Background

General context

The baseline measurement of administrative burdens on business showed that some 40% of burdens can be traced back to EU-origin regulation (partly or fully), including a number of significant policy areas (such as VAT, company law and rules on accounting and reporting, working environment, public procurement and food safety). Measurements for burdens on citizens suggest that 23% of these burdens in terms of time, and 15% in terms of costs, have their origin at EU level.

Negotiating EU regulations

Institutional framework and processes

All European Commission regulatory and policy proposals[3] are discussed (as soon as the texts are available) within the Working Group for the Assessment of New Commission Proposals (BNC – *Beoordeling Nieuwe Commissievoorstellen*). Each ministry has a representative on this committee, which is chaired by a senior official of the Ministry of Foreign Affairs. The committee determines the lead ministry for negotiation and subsequent transposition of the proposal, and which other ministries should be involved.

The committee also starts the process of developing a Dutch position, focusing on proportionality and subsidiarity. Regulatory implications for the subnational levels of government or regulatory agencies are also taken into consideration at this stage. The Association of Netherlands Municipalities (VNG) and the Association of Provinces (IPO) are members. They do not always attend but take a particular interest in environmental

Figure 7.1. Structure of EU decision-making

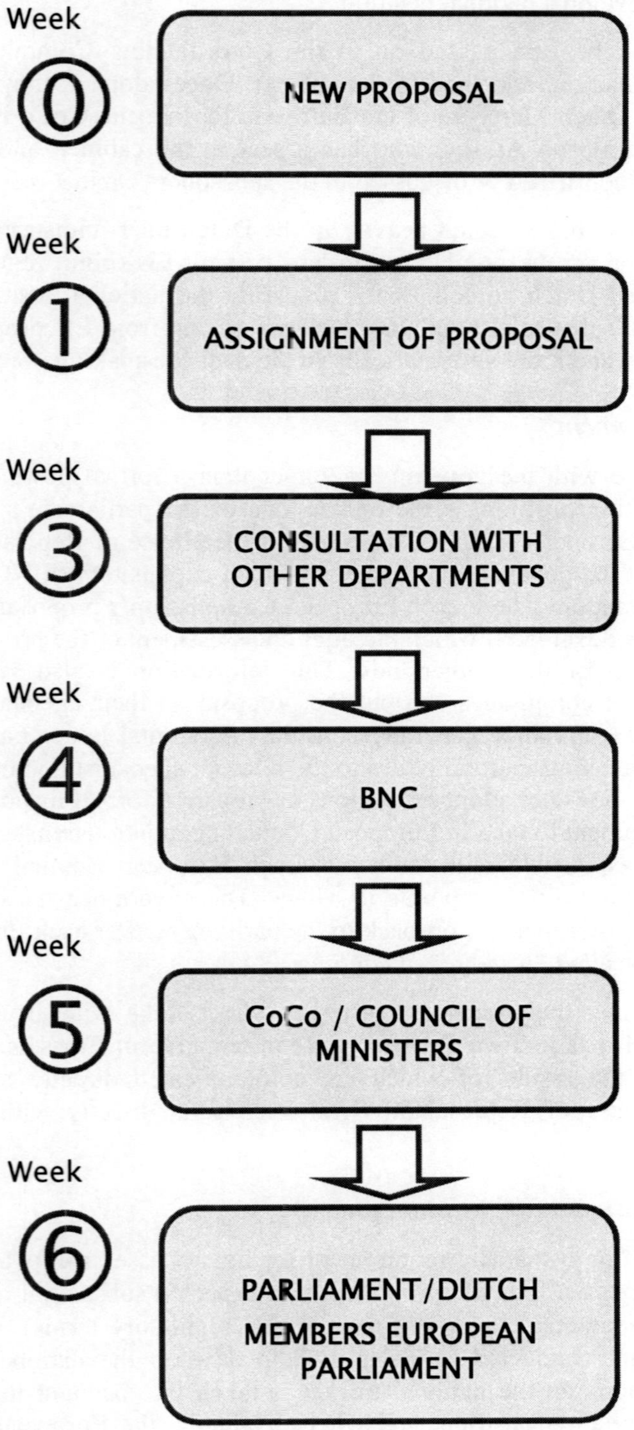

issues.[4] If there is an agency angle, the parent ministry is also involved, if it is not already. A co-ordinated initial Dutch position is prepared by specialists from the ministries involved. A special form ("BNC-fiche") is used to assess each proposal of the European Commission and to develop a national position.

Completed draft fiches are passed on to the Co-ordinating Committee (CoCo) for discussion and confirmation, and then to the cabinet. Once adopted, they are sent to the parliament and to the Dutch Members of the European Parliament. CoCo is chaired by the State Secretary for European Affairs, who has a seat in the cabinet, and meets weekly. CoCo conclusions are confirmed or discussed in the subsequent cabinet meeting.

Since 2007 the RRG has invested heavily in the Dutch inter-ministerial framework in order to focus attention on the regulatory burdens of new EU-origin regulations. This is reflected in the revised Dutch guidelines for preparing the national position on new EU proposals. As a result, substantial regulatory burdens arising from EU proposals are being addressed much earlier and more systematically in the decision-making process.

The role of the parliament

Influential dialogue with the government, rather than a formal power to confirm the government's negotiating position, is the cornerstone of the parliament's engagement on EU legislation.[5] The European Affairs Committee of the House of Representatives is sent draft EU proposals by the government, together with an explanatory "BNC-fiche" (a form of explanatory memorandum where each European Commission's proposal is assessed and the national position is developed) which includes an assessment of the proposal's financial and other implications for the Netherlands. This information is also sent to the other committees. Any of the committees can put the proposal on their agenda for discussion. The European Affairs Committee generally considers horizontal issues (such as the EU's constitutional future), leaving sectoral issues to the relevant specialist committee. Generally speaking, a committee does not adopt resolutions or prepare a formal mandate setting out a position for the government to take in European Council negotiations. Instead, it engages in discussion with the responsible minister before each European Council meeting, in the expectation that the latter will incorporate its views. The government is motivated to pay attention, since the minister must report back to the parliament after each European Council meeting (this is the so-called "*principle of confidence*").

It is noteworthy that the parliament also has direct links with Brussels and other national parliaments. It has its own Permanent Representative in Brussels. It carries out a "subsidiarity check", the results of which are communicated directly to the European Commission. The House of Representatives also consults directly with other national parliaments.[6]

Ex ante impact assessment (negotiation phase)

There is no formal or systematic requirement for impact assessments to be carried out on EU regulatory proposals.[7] For EU proposals with expected substantial repercussions on the national situation (among others in financial and regulatory terms), special national impact assessments are conducted in order to help develop the national position. The impact of EU regulations on the national market is taken into account in the BNC-fiche underpinning the negotiating position, and where available, the European Commission's impact assessment is attached to the fiche. Certain environmental proposals are the subject of a separate procedure.

Transposing EU regulations

Institutional framework and processes

Transposition rests on two principles responsibility of the lead policy ministry, backed up by a centralised monitoring structure to track progress.

Responsibility for the transposition of EU regulations (as in most other EU countries) lies with the relevant policy ministry, reflecting the view that "Europe" should be integrated into national policy and law making. The responsibility includes the correct and timely implementation of EU regulations at subnational level or by a regulatory agency. It also covers the removal of discrepancies resulting from existing national regulations.

Transposition is co-ordinated and monitored by ICER (*Interdepartementale commissie Europees recht* – Interdepartmental Commission for European Law) and a subcommission of ICER, ICER-I, under the aegis of the Ministry of Justice.[8] All ministries participate in these commissions. As soon as an EU regulation has been adopted, the lead ministry formulates an implementation plan, which is put to ICER-I. The plan, which includes a timeframe for the various steps and actions, may be amended to take account of comments from other ministries.

Dutch policy seeks to avoid mixing up the implementation of EU regulations with the pursuit of national policies. The general rule has been that legislation to implement EU regulations should not be used or extended to cover national policy issues, in order to avoid implementation delays. This cannot, however, always be prevented. The rule also does not preclude separate proposals for legislation related to national policy needs.

Guidance and support

Guidance material is produced by ICER. Reports, guidelines and other sources of information are published on the websites of the Centre of Expertise for European Law (*Expertise centrum Europees recht*- ECER), and of the Knowledge Centre for Legislation (*Kenniscentrum wetgeving*).[9] Also available are the so-called "Answers to the most frequently asked questions about the implementation of EU regulations (*Praktijkvragen over de implementatie van EG-besluiten*"), which is currently being updated.

Legal provisions and the role of the parliament

There is no special legislative tool for transposition of EU regulations. National legislative procedures are generally simplified with respect to legislation that (solely) serves to implement EU regulations. Article 1.7 of the General Administrative Law (*Algemene wet bestuursrecht*) stipulates that legal obligations to consult stakeholders are not applicable with respect to EU-related implementation. Consultation may nevertheless take place if it is considered necessary and useful, in particular when significant discretion is left as to how member states may transpose an EU regulation.

Ex ante impact assessment (transposition phase)

Implementation proposals are subject to simplified impact assessment procedures on the assumption that there is little room for debate at that stage. The impact on business, promoted by the RRG, is the most important feature of this check.

Monitoring transposition

Implementation plans adopted by ICER-I are immediately entered into an electronic database, the I-Timer. This database covers deadlines for implementation, as well as normative dates for the steps that need to be taken in the legislative process. The database thus reveals whether implementation deadlines have been met (or expired). Every quarter a report on the state of implementation results is sent to the parliament's European Affairs Committee by the State Secretary for European Affairs. This sets out which regulations have been implemented and which are pending. If the implementation deadline is or will likely be exceeded the reasons are given. Although there is no national database of transposition rates, at the end of each year an overview of implementation rates compared with previous years is given. This shows that implementation performance is steadily improving in terms of both numbers and average delay period.

Speed of transposition

The speed of transposition varies considerably depending on the issue (as does the implementation period given in the EU regulation) and on the legal instrument used for implementation. It was explained that there are rules of thumb, however, about the period it generally takes to implement an EU regulation depending on whether this requires a law (18 months), decree (6 months) or ministerial regulation (3 months). The Netherlands records a very good comparative performance on transposition, according to the EU's Internal Market Scoreboard, which ranks it third among the EU 15 countries. A recent review by the NCA, however, came to a less positive conclusion.

Box 7.1. Netherlands performance in the transposition of EU Directives

The EU Internal Market Scoreboard

The Netherlands performs very well, ranking third among the EU-15 countries. It shows a transposition deficit of 0.8%. This is considerably lower than a few years ago (the deficit was 2-3% until 2000).

The level of transposition is particularly low in the fields of Justice, Freedom and Security. There are also low levels of transposition in Energy and Transport.

NL	Nov-97	May-98	Nov-98	May-99	Nov-99	May-00	Nov-00	May-01	Nov-01	May-02
Transposition deficit as % in terms of Internal Market Directives	3.5	2.2	2.1	2.4	2.8	3	2.5	2	1.3	1.3
	Nov-02	May-03	Jul-04	Jul-05	Dec-05	Jul-06	Nov-06	Jul-07	Nov-07	Jul-08
	1.3	2	2.8	1.6	1.2	1.5	1	1.6	0.7	0.8

The conclusions of the Netherlands Court of Audit[1]

The NCA carried out an audit of Dutch transposition performance in 2008.[2] The audit confirms that there are deficits in transposition. In 2001 and 2006, the Netherlands had to transpose 539 directives into national law. 51 per cent were transposed late. In 2007, almost half the directives were transposed beyond the time limit. The proportion of directives transposed beyond the deadline rose to over three-quarters when implementation required the involvement of more than one Ministry.[3]

However, there was also a decline in the number of days between the deadline set for transposition, and the date on which the directives were finally transposed. From 2002 to 2005, the average length of the delay fell from 383 to 142 days. However, the average length of the delay rose again in 2006, to 162 days.[4]

Contrary to the conclusions from the EU data used, the NCA does not make out a clear trend of transposition performance. According to their result, between 2001 and 2007, half of the directives are transposed too late, ranging from 45-60%.[5] Other data, for instance those regarding the transposition of social policy directives, also suggest a lower level of transposition speed than one that could be deduced from the EU data. Here the Netherlands transposes only about two fifths of the social policy directives in time.[6]

Notes

1. The Ministries of Justice and Foreign Affairs have commented on the findings of the NCA in a letter to the parliament dated 15-10-2008. In this letter they state that the data used by the NCA show a clear improvement over the given time period when corrected for a distorting factor that the NCA had not taken into account.
2. *www.rekenkamer.nl/9282000/d/p447_european_legislation.pdf.*
3. Netherlands Court of Auditors 2008: 61. Where more than one ministry is involved in the transposition, the average length of the delay is 40 weeks. The average length of delay where just one ministry is responsible for transposition is 34 weeks.
4. For all these data cf. Netherlands Court of Audit 2008: 8.
5. Mastenbroek 2003: 384. She also finds corresponding lower transposition levels for the NL than the EU data suggest even seeing a structural transposition deficit as regards the NL.
6. Haverland/ Romeijn 2006: 12.

Correlation with national regulations

Legislation to implement EU regulations has to state the correlation between the provisions in the national and the EU regulation. To this end, a correlation table should be included in the BNC-fiche that accompanies the proposal, although this does not always happen, in which case the fiche states *verbatim* the relationship between the national and EU regulation.

Double-banking[10]

Consistency of national legislation with EU regulations is an element of the legal quality framework promulgated by the Ministry of Justice. Legal quality checks of proposed national legislation by the Ministry of Justice and the Council of State (see Chapter 4) pay close attention to possible inconsistencies between national and European law. In addition, another sub-commission of ICER, ICER-H[11] monitors the jurisprudence of the European courts for any decision that may show the need for amendment of national legislation or practices.

Gold plating[12]

Part of the business impact assessment for new EU-origin regulations is expected to consider the issue of gold plating. In 2006 an inventory was completed of 105 complaints about gold plating, of which 16 were considered to have some foundation. Most of these are currently being addressed.

Interface with Better Regulation at EU level

The Netherlands have been active for some years in working with the European Commission and other member states to promote Better Regulation. Particular efforts have gone into promoting policies to reduce administrative burdens, both for business and for citizens, and the Netherlands have made a number of specific recommendations for tangible burden reduction linked to specific reduction targets to the European Commission, emphasising the need for a three-pronged approach for business burdens: give the policy more strategic prominence in the context of the Lisbon agenda for growth and competitiveness; prevent new EU burdens; and tackle burdens in existing EU regulations.

As regards the citizen agenda, there have been significant recent efforts by the Ministry of Interior to raise awareness with the European Commission and other member states over the EU origin of many citizen-related burdens, and it has established an informal European network on the issues.

Notes

1. Not to be confused with the generic use of the term "regulation" for this project.
2. The World Bank's 2007 report had this to say about the Dutch work at EU level: "Dutch leadership on BR in the EU can be deepened. Significant effort has gone into getting Brussels to understand the benefits of simpler regulation. High-level political prioritisation during the 2004 Dutch Presidency. Increased focus on admin burdens in the review of EU regulations. Secondment of Dutch staff to the Commission. Informal networks such as Directors of Better Regulation and SCM network. Dissemination efforts also in the OECD and World Bank. Netherlands played a lead role in the adoption by the EU of 25% reduction target. Continuing efforts are important. More active lobbying early in the process, working with the Foreign Affairs ministry on the negotiating position."
3. Including important proposals from member states regarding title VI of the EU Treaty.
4. VNG also has 44 lobbyists in Brussels.
5. In some countries such as the United Kingdom, the parliament's engagement includes a formal process of agreeing the government's negotiation position for Council.
6. For example through interparliamentary conferences such as COSAC (Conference of Community and European Affairs Committees of Parliaments of the European Union), or through websites like IPEX (Inter-parliamentary EU Information Exchange Commission).
7. There is no reference to EU regulations in the current impact assessment guidance.
8. "I" stands for Implementation.
9. *www.minbuza.ecer.nl. www.kc-wetgeving.nl.*
10. Avoiding situations where EU legislation covers the same ground as national legislation.
11. For *Hof* – meaning court.
12. Over implementation of an EC directive through the imposition of national requirements going beyond the requirements of the directive. Directives allow member states to choose how to meet the objectives set out in the directive, adapting their approach to their own institutional and administrative cultures. It is often at this stage that additional details and refinements, not directly prescribed by the directive, are introduced. These can go well beyond the requirements of the directive, resulting in extra costs and burdens.

Chapter 8

The interface between subnational and national levels of government

Multilevel regulatory governance- that is to say, taking into account the rule-making and rule-enforcement activities of all the different levels of government, not just the national level – is another core element of effective regulatory management. The OECD's 2005 *Guiding Principles for Regulatory Quality and Performance* "encourage Better Regulation at all levels of government, improved co-ordination, and the avoidance of overlapping responsibilities among regulatory authorities and levels of government". It is relevant to all countries that are seeking to improve their regulatory management, whether they are federations, unitary states or somewhere in between.

In many countries local governments are entrusted with a large number of complex tasks, covering important parts of the welfare system and public services such as social services, health care and education, as well as housing, planning and building issues, and environmental protection. Licensing can be a key activity at this level. These issues have a direct impact on the welfare of businesses and citizens. Local governments within the boundaries of a state need increasing flexibility to meet economic, social and environmental goals in their particular geographical and cultural setting. At the same time, they may be taking on a growing responsibility for the implementation of EC regulations. All of this requires a pro active consideration of:

- The allocation/sharing of regulatory responsibilities at the different levels of government (which can be primary rule-making responsibilities; secondary rule-making responsibilities based on primary legislation, or the transposition of EC regulations; responsibilities for supervision/enforcement of national or subnational regulations; or responsibilities for service delivery).
- The capacities of these different levels to produce quality regulation.
- The co-ordination mechanisms between the different levels, and across the same levels.

Assessment and recommendations

Considerable effort and resources are being put into linking up the local level with national objectives for Better Regulation, and results have started to emerge. There is increasing co-operation between central and local levels of government in key areas of Better Regulation such as reform of inspection practices, the reduction of administrative burdens and licensing reform. Core ministries (Interior, Finance and Economic Affairs) are clearly working hard to involve local governments in their Better Regulation programmes.

Central government is providing direct support for municipalities, including consultancy funds to address burden reductions. Concrete results have started to emerge such as the review and simplification of "model regulations" (templates for local regulations produced by the Association of Municipalities VNG), the establishment of a Better Regulation website dedicated to local level Better Regulation issues, and pilot schemes to test the principle of "silence is consent" for licensing.

The Central Government Agreement with the Municipalities is an effective means of structuring the approach and identifying priorities. This agreement (under which a specific action plan is drawn up), which is concluded between central government and the VNG at the start of each government term, has been used to good effect to define shared goals.

Uneven progress can be expected and the role of the VNG is important for evening out differences across the country. With 441 municipalities (a large number for a relatively small country) and considerable variations in size (and culture), some municipalities are doing better than others. The OECD peer review team were told that progress on licensing reform is especially patchy. The role of the VNG is important for disseminating best practice and encouraging horizontal co-operation.

The action plan rightly addresses not only what municipalities can do for central government but also what central government can do for municipalities. The task force for addressing burdens generated by central government (part of the action plan) addresses the important issue of regulatory burdens generated by central government. There is concern at the local level at the weight of new regulations and a desire to see more targeted management of the development of new regulations which will "hit" the local level. The VNG has proposed that each ministry appoint a co-ordinating lawyer for new regulation that will affect the local level.

Recommendation 8.1. Further development of the shared agenda for Better Regulation should pay particular attention to licensing, and to finding effective ways of addressing the likely impact of centrally generated regulations on the local level. This issue should be included in the proposed review of *ex ante* impact assessment (see Chapter 4).

Background

Structure, responsibilities and funding of local governments

Structure of local governments

Provinces and municipalities

The Netherlands is a decentralised unitary state with three tiers of government. It is divided into 12 provinces[1] and 441 municipalities.[2] Each province and municipality has its own council, elected by popular vote. Their executives are chaired by provincial governors (Queen's commissioners) and mayors, who are appointed by the central government, and who also chair their council. They can be established, dissolved, and their boundaries can be revised by act of the parliament. The Ministry of Interior has overall co-ordinating responsibility for local government affairs.

There are significant differences in size and culture between municipalities. The "big four" cover the four main cities of Amsterdam, Den Haag, Utrecht, and Rotterdam.[3] These interact directly with central government ministries. The Association of Netherlands

Municipalities (VNG) speaks on behalf of the smaller municipalities. The capacities of smaller municipalities for Better Regulation is very limited.

Water boards

In addition, there are water boards, which are responsible for water management. The water boards are one of the oldest democratic institutions in the Netherlands. Water management is an important issue as about one quarter of the Netherlands lies below sea level. The boards are public bodies, with executive councils elected for the most part by property owners in their localities. The chair of the executive committee is appointed by the central government.

Responsibilities and powers of local governments

Provincial and municipal authorities have important implementation and enforcement (including inspection) functions, especially in physical and environmental planning, and in licensing, based on regulations laid down by central government. Most inspections are carried out by local governments, except for food, health and safety, labour issues. Municipalities are also required to implement certain measures laid down by the province to which they belong.

Provinces and municipalities also have limited powers to make their own regulations (by-laws) on matters that directly affect them, and they may also make additional regulations in areas that have already been regulated at national level. Provincial executives implement a number of central government regulations in joint governance. The Constitution and the Municipal Act set the framework for local rule- making. The General Municipal Ordinance contains most of the local regulation.

Provincial authorities are responsible for environmental management, spatial planning, energy supply, social work, sport and cultural affairs. They also play a co-ordinating and planning role, and supervise the finances of the municipalities.

Municipal authorities are responsible for water supply, traffic, housing, public authority schools, social services, health care, sport, recreation, and culture.

Funding of local governments

Provinces and municipalities have two main sources of income: local taxes and charges which amount to some 19% of total income for municipalities,[4] and central government funding. Most of the latter is in the form of ring-fenced special purpose grants. In addition, municipalities receive block grants from the provinces and municipalities funds which they can spend as they see fit. Municipalities draft their budget annually on the basis of the Budget and Accountability Decree for Provinces and Municipalities.

Better Regulation policies deployed at local level

Central Government Agreement with the Municipalities

The centrepiece of Better Regulation at the local level is an agreement ("*Bestuursakkoord*"), which is made at the start of its term of office by central government with the Association of Netherlands Municipalities VNG (of which all Dutch municipalities are members) to follow up on relevant aspects of the Coalition Agreement. The current central-local agreement requires a reduction of 25% in administrative burdens from municipalities for citizens and companies. It also requires that administrative burdens between government levels should be reduced by 25%. The VNG and central government have developed an action plan to give effect to this agreement.

Box 8.1. Action plan for the reduction of administrative burdens at local level

- *Review of model regulations.* Model regulations are produced by VNG when new policies must be implemented by municipalities. Because municipalities do not always have the judicial knowledge or capacity, VNG produce model regulations which can easily be implemented by municipalities. Following consultation with stakeholders, and using a form of the Standard Cost Model, the VNG has reduced the number of model regulations from 147 to 117, including a review to make them more "administrative burden friendly". A number of e-forms for online use have also been developed to promote uniform implementation by municipalities.

- *Central-local taskforce for addressing burdens generated by central government.* This brings together central government representatives and the VNG, and is chaired by a high-profile mayor.[5] Problems identified by the Task Force may be relayed directly to the responsible central government State Secretary. The VNG has produced a list of national regulations which are seen as an obstacle to the reduction of administrative burdens at local level. The 2006 State of Local Government Report calculates that on average, municipalities receive a ministerial circular every second working day.[6] The baseline measurement of administrative burdens on business showed that around 90% of the administrative burdens of municipalities originate from tasks delegated to municipalities from the national government based on national regulations. Only 10% of administrative burdens thus originate from the autonomous competences of municipalities.

- *Simplification of central government payments to municipalities.* Replacing specific payments by central government for the execution of tasks delegated to the municipal level by payment to a common municipal Fund. Municipalities will no longer have to report on expenditure linked to specific payments.

- *Website.* Funded by the Interior, Finance and Economic Affairs ministries, and run by the VNG, the website describes how municipalities can reduce the administrative burdens for citizens and companies ("less rules, more service").[7]

- *Consultancy funds.* Possibility for municipalities to apply for a facility to receive a small payment for hiring a consultant (it will compensate 75% of the total costs), who can measure the administrative burdens caused by this specific municipality and give advice on measures which can be taken to reduce these burdens. In this way, municipalities become aware of the administrative burdens they cause in their own municipality. This facility is financed by the ministries of Finance, Economic Affairs and the Interior.

- *Top ten bottlenecks for citizens.* Municipalities are involved in the top ten bottlenecks for citizens. Pilot projects are being started in the field of volunteers and mediation. Others will follow. *Pioneer municipalities.* A group of pioneer municipalities have been created, which are very active in the field of reducing administrative burdens. Best practices are disseminated on the website hosted by the VNG.

- *Trailblazers.* There are also some 80 trailblazer municipalities involved in pilot schemes to test whether *lex silencio* can be applied.

The VNG drew particular attention to the reform of model regulations but it also noted that making model regulations more administrative burden friendly raises the issue of a new approach to risk. "To what extent are politicians and society willing to accept risks? The last decades had an almost risk-free society Acceptance of a certain level of public risk will be decisive for success. We have to make politicians aware of the possibility of organizing society in other ways than with regulation."[8]

Initiatives by specific municipalities

This largely depends on the size of municipalities. Some larger municipalities are particularly active on their own account and in the framework of national policy on Better Regulation. For example, Amsterdam has set itself Better Regulation goals, which are set out in its annual report, and has established a steering group of its (very autonomous) district councils to oversee progress. It was the recipient of a European e-Government award in recognition of its efforts to streamline licensing procedures, and is making substantial efforts to reform its inspection approach in line with the national policy of more proportionate and information based inspections (including a training academy for inspectors). It notes that RRG also helps and monitors progress.

Consultation and communication

The VNG draws attention to a number of mechanisms aimed at ensuring that stakeholders (including administrators within local government) are aware of, and can comment on, Better Regulation developments:

- Regulations made by local governments are systematically communicated to affected parties and to citizens in general.

- A Better Regulation website hosted by the VNG has been established (less rules more service), dedicated to the dissemination of information on Better Regulation projects at the local level.[9]

- Efforts are made to ensure that communication approaches are tailored to the audience: brochures, instruction manuals, newsletters, articles in national and local newspapers, seminars, workshops, meetings, conferences.

- Specific initiatives such as the reform of model regulations and the local level's engagement in the regulatory burden reduction programmes are discussed with local stakeholders and feedback given to them.

Co-ordination mechanisms

Co-ordination between the national and municipal levels, as well as co-ordination between municipalities, is assured by the Association of Netherlands Municipalities (VNG). The Association of Provincial Authorities (IPO – *Inter-Provinciaal Overleg*) represents the provincial level. The IPO's activities reflect the competences of the provinces, namely the environment, rural affairs, social policy, regional development, housing, culture, water, security and enforcement, mobility and the economy.

Box 8.2. Association of Netherlands Municipalities (VNG)

The Association of Netherlands Municipalities (VNG) is the main organisation representing Dutch municipalities. It was originally established in 1912 by 28 Dutch cities. Membership is voluntary but by 1950 all municipalities had become members *check.* It is funded by the municipalities.

The VNG covers the following activities:

- Representation, negotiation and consultation on municipalities' interests with central government (notably the Ministry of Interior and the RRG for the regulatory burden reduction programmes), as well as with the provincial level, the EU institutions and other relevant public bodies.
- It represents municipalities' interests in negotiations on collective labour agreements with unions of local government personnel.
- Advice and information to members on issues of local interest.
- Together with *Egem* (an organisation that works on electronic tools for municipalities) supply of electronic forms for model regulations. Encouragement and support to municipalities to improve their electronic access and electronic payments.
- Provision of services for municipalities, including model regulations. Dissemination of best practice.

Notes

1. Groningen, Friesland, Drenthe, Overijssel, Gelderland, Utrecht, North Holland, South Holland, Zeeland, North Brabant, Limburg, Flevoland.
2. As of January 2009.
3. Economic activity in the Netherlands is concentrated in the area known as the Randstad, the urban belt that includes the country's four main cities.
4. Property tax, court fees, local charges such as dog licences.
5. The mayor of Groningen, who is also well known in national politics.
6. According to the report, a circular can be understood as a general written communication from central government to all provinces or municipalities, which may relate to new regulations, detailed explanations of regulations, instructions regarding the discretionary interpretation of regulations, or requests for co-operation.
7. *www.minderregelsmeerservice.nl/smartsite.*
8. Reply to OECD questionnaire.
9. *www.minderregelsmeerservice.nl.*

Bibliography

ACTAL (2006), Annual report, The Hague.

Ministry of Economic Affairs (2006), "Handbook on Substantive Compliance Costs for the Business World in respect of proposed regulations", A.F.M. Nijsen, P.A.van der Hauw, G.Regter, The Hague.

Netherlands Court of Audit (2003), "Strategy 2004-2009".

Netherlands Government (2007 and 2008), "Lisbon Strategy for Growth and Jobs- Netherlands National Reform Programme", The Hague.

Netherlands Government/Ministry of Justice (2003), "Assessment of Proposed Regulation, guidelines", The Hague.

Netherlands Government/Ministry of the Interior and Kingdom Relations (2007), "Inspection Simplification Programme: End of year report", The Hague.

Netherlands Government/Ministry of the Interior and Kingdom Relations (2007), "Action Plan Top Ten Bottlenecks", The Hague.

Netherlands Government/Ministry of the Interior and Kingdom Relations (2006), "Noticeably Less and Better: process evaluation report on administrative burden reduction for citizens", The Hague.

Netherlands Government/Regulatory Reform Group (2007), "Action Plan Reduction of Red Tape for Businesses 2007-2011", The Hague.

Netherlands Government/Regulatory Reform Group (2008), "Noticeably less: integrated progress report on the programme for the reduction of administrative burdens", report to Parliament, The Hague.

Netherlands Government/Regulatory Reform Group (2008), "Progress report, regulatory burdens on businesses", The Hague.

Netherlands Government/Regulatory Reform Group (2009), "Communication Plan", The Hague.

OECD (2007), *OECD e-Government Studies: Netherlands*, OECD Publishing, Paris.

OECD (1999), *OECD Reviews of Regulatory Reform: Regulatory Reform in the Netherlands*, OECD Publishing, Paris.

OECD (2007), *Cutting Red Tape: Administrative Simplification in the Netherlands*, OECD Publishing, Paris.

OECD (2008), *Economic Survey: Netherlands*, OECD Publishing, Paris.

World Bank (2007), *Review of Dutch Administrative Burden Reduction Programme*, World Bank Group, Washington DC.

Annex A. General institutional context for the Dutch policy, law making and law execution process

General framework

The Kingdom of the Netherlands, as it is officially known, is a parliamentary constitutional monarchy with the monarch as head of state.[1] It consists of three countries: Aruba, the Netherlands Antilles and the Netherlands. Under the rules laid down in the Constitution, the government, including the Prime Minister, is formed jointly by the monarch and the ministers of the current administration.[2] Responsibility for the government's actions is, however, borne by ministers. The hereditary monarchy operates in conjunction with a democratic parliamentary system, under which Members of the parliament are elected by the people. Amsterdam is the capital of the Netherlands, but the seat of the head of state and the government is in the Hague.

The Dutch Constitution, known as the *grondwet* (basic law), dates back to 1814, when the Kingdom was established, and has been amended many times since.[3] Alongside the *grondwet* there exists a body of accepted uncodified principles which play an important part in the functioning of the political and judicial system.

The executive

Structure

There are thirteen ministries.[4] Each ministry is headed by a minister (sometimes two), supported by one or more secretaries of state. Ministers cannot at the same time be members of the parliament. The government can also appoint as ministers individuals who have not stood for office. Individual ministers can be voted down by the parliament without consequences for the government as a whole. The civil service is politically neutral.

As in most other OECD countries decision-making is collective, based on a network of ministerial committees, ultimately reporting to the Council of Ministers, which meets weekly. Policy proposals go to the relevant ministerial committees, after discussions at official level. Policy must be adopted collectively.

Coalition agreements and the planning cycle

The government works on the basis of coalition agreements (*Coalitieakkoord*) which set the policy framework for the four years of the electoral cycle, and annual budget plans. Together these generate proposals for policy/legislation. The annual planning and reporting cycle starts with the government's Annual Budget Memorandum and Ministerial Budgets to the parliament (September) and concludes with annual reports to the parliament on the past year (May). The current coalition government was formed after the elections of November 2006. The Cabinet was installed on 22 February 2007. New elections for the House of Representatives are planned on 11 May 2011.

The current coalition agreement includes six pillars (supported by 70 goals) that form the basis for government policy for the four years of the election cycle, and to promote shared objectives and interaction between ministries:

- An active role internationally and in Europe.

- An innovative, competitive and dynamic economy.
- A sustainable environment to make the world better than we found it.
- Social cohesion, because every person counts and everyone is needed.
- Safety, stability and respect, the basis for mutual trust.
- A decisive government that stands by its citizens and binds them together, and a public sector dedicated to serving them.

Regulatory agencies

As in other OECD countries, central government is supported in its work by a variety of regulatory agencies. Dutch regulatory agencies can be divided into three main groups:

- Agencies (*agentschappen*). These are essentially specialised executive agencies for the enforcement (with limited discretion) of policies and regulations set by their parent Ministry. The latter is ultimately accountable for their work and decisions. They have their own executive and budget. The 14 national inspectorates (*inspectie*) are the most important subcategory.[5] These inspectorates are set up according to a common template as regards budget and legal arrangements, although their tasks and responsibilities vary. The Ministry of Interior has a systemic/co-ordination responsibility for inspections policy, but not for the work and underlying policy objectives for individual inspectorates.

- Autonomous administrative bodies (*zelfstandige bestuursorganen – ZBO*). Their tasks and responsibilities are defined in a primary law or order in council. Their legal status varies (they can be public or private bodies), as does the work they carry out. Their tasks generally require the strict and independent application of regulations in individual cases, often by independent experts, for example the issue of licences, or quality checks, which they perform at arm's length of their parent Ministry (which appoints their board, issues general instructions and approves their budget). The parent ministry is not accountable for their decisions. There are 140 *check* ZBOs. They include the chambers of commerce, the Centre for Work and Income, the Competition Authority, and the Bank of the Netherlands.

- Statutory trade agencies (*openbare lichamen voor beroep en bedrijf – STAs*). These are public bodies for industry and the professions, recognised by the government and with statutory powers. They have corporatist bipartite governing boards, and draw up agreements and regulations for specific economic sectors and professional groups. They are in effect a form of alternative regulation. The main category comprises public law regulatory bodies (*publiekrechtelijke bestuursorganen*), and the most important is the Social and Economic Council (SER), which brings together representatives of employers and employees with government appointed members, to promote the interests of the national economy and business community. The SER's recommendations to government carry considerable weight, especially if they have the unanimous support of all its members.[6] There are also several public bodies for the professions (including lawyers, accountants, ship pilots). These too have the power to issue ordinances, which are only binding on the organisation's own members.

The legislature[7]

Structure

The Dutch parliament – known as the States General (*Staten-Generaal*) has two chambers. The Senate (the upper house – *Eerste Kamer*) has 75 part-time members, who are elected for a term of four years by the members of the twelve provincial councils, who are in turn directly elected by the inhabitants of the provinces. The 150 members of the House of Representatives (the lower house – *Tweede Kamer)* are directly elected by the people, also for a four-year term. They are full-time politicians. The main purpose of the legislature (as in other democratic systems) is to control the executive and hold the government to account for its actions.

Elections

Elections are based on a system of proportional representation, under which each party is allocated a number of seats in the parliament corresponding to the proportion of the overall vote won by that party. Because of the large number of political parties resulting from this system the country is always governed by coalitions. No single political party has ever obtained an outright parliamentary majority. There is currently a coalition majority in the parliament.[8]

The House of Representatives

The House of Representatives has considerably greater powers than the Senate. It is responsible for enacting all new legislation and for approving amendments to existing legislation. It has the following powers:

- The right of legislative initiative –it can submit bills on its own initiative. Bills proposed by the government are, however, the most common form. There are no hard figures about the actual number but it is estimated that 85-90% of all legislative proposals put before the parliament are proposed by the government. There is some indication that the number of proposals by members of the parliament has risen in the last 2-3 years. Proposals by members of the parliament tend to be withdrawn or rejected more often than government proposals: at least 95% of all proposals that make it to actual laws were proposed by government.

- The right to amend draft legislation proposed by the government. The relevant minister may adopt or reject the amendment, but in the latter case and if the House of Representatives wishes to keep the amendment, the minister has two choices: to withdraw the draft, or threaten to resign.

- The right to ask questions. Questions (written or oral – via a weekly "question time" session) may be put to members of the cabinet by individual members of the House of Representatives.

- The right of interpellation. This is the right to ask the cabinet for information, which often gives rise to a debate. Debates provide an opportunity to ask questions on issues that cannot be covered by questions.

- The right to submit motions. If a member of the House of Representatives disagrees with part of government policy s/he can table a motion which obliges the House to make a statement on the issue. A general motion of no confidence in the government may also be tabled. The House only votes on a motion if it is supported by at least four other members.

- The right to approve the national budget. The process allows the House to raise or lower the amount, and make adjustments to specific spending plans.

- The right to establish an inquiry. Both the House of Representatives and the Senate have this right, jointly and separately. An inquiry must be set up by act of the parliament. This right has been exercised several times in recent years.

The committee system for the House of Representatives consists of:

- Standing committees (one for each ministry, apart from the Ministry of General Affairs, for European Affairs, and Netherlands Antilles and Aruba Affairs).

- General committees, which can be appointed "for subjects which are of special importance" to the House or which concern all ministers.

- Theme committees, which are concerned with topics of great social importance which cut across ministry boundaries.

- Temporary Committees, for specific issues.

- Committee for Public Expenditure. This committee supervises the correct expenditure of the budget resources by the government. It also advises other parliamentary committees on issues budget accountability procedures major (infrastructural) projects.

- Board of enquiry. A special temporary committee is the so called "parliamentary board of enquiry". These boards are appointed by the House of Representatives if an enquiry of a special matter is wished for. These boards of enquiry have the authority to interrogate witnesses under oath and witnesses are obliged to appear for the board.

The Senate

- The Senate also scrutinises the government's actions, but in more of an advisory capacity. Formally, it can only accept or reject draft legislation in its entirety i.e. it cannot amend a bill. Its approval is required for the enactment of a bill, but rejection is a rare event. It also discusses the national budget, but again, has no powers to propose amendments. The Senate has no right to initiate legislation. It has the right to put questions and propose motions as well as (see above) to establish an inquiry.

The judiciary

The legal system

The Dutch judicial system is based on the traditions of continental Europe, with a codified law and a written constitution. When a law is enacted by the legislature, it cannot be directly challenged by the judiciary. However the courts can and do interpret the law.

The Council of State[9]

The Council of State (*Raad van State*) is a form of constitutional court, advising the government on all draft bills and royal decrees (orders in council). Members are former politicians, judges, scholars, and civil servants, with permanent appointments until the age of 70. Although its advice is not formally binding, it carries considerable weight, as the government regularly amends bills on its advice. The Council of State is also the court of appeal for disputes relating to administrative law (between organs of state and between an organ of state and a private individual or company). It is made up of 26 members and the monarch.

The Council for the Judiciary[10]

The Council for the Judiciary was founded in 2002 to promote the quality of the judicial system, including the uniform application of the law, and to provide operational support for the judicial system. It advises the government and the parliament about new laws which have implications for the judicial system, in ongoing consultation with the courts. It also advises on the policy which central government should pursue in respect of the administration of justice. Its advice is formulated in ongoing consultation with the courts. The Council is also responsible for the judiciary system's budget, and for the recruitment, selection and training of judicial and court officials. The Council has a support office of about 120 people.

The court system

The Netherlands court system consists of courts (*rechtbanken*), courts of appeal (*gerechsthof*) and a Supreme Court (*Hoge Raad*), the latter two only for civil and criminal cases.

Administrative appeals are heard by the administrative branch of the courts, and in appeal by specific administrative courts.[11] Appeals are always preceded by an objection procedure (*bezwaar*) with the body that took the initial decision.

All courts rule on the interpretation of regulations, except for the Supreme Court, which rules on procedure, and interpretation based solely on the facts of the case.

Other key actors at the central level

The Netherlands Court of Audit

The Netherlands Court of Audit (NCA – *Algemene Rekenkamer*) provides *ex post* scrutiny of government actions. It investigates whether public funds have been collected and spent legitimately, efficiently and effectively. It is independent of the government and the parliament.[12] Its three board members are appointed for life. It decides for itself what to audit, how to do so and what to publish, although it considers requests from the government and the parliament. That said it considers the parliament, to which it is ultimately accountable for its own management, to be its main "customer", and it seeks to gear its work programme to meet the needs of the parliament. It publishes an annual programme of audit projects. Reports set out factual findings, and make recommendations for improvement. It does not take political positions, for example to say that a law is "not good", though it may say that a law is not working the way it was intended. Some reports of recent years have been very critical of the failure to implement agreed government policies effectively. The NCA does not audit local government.

The NCA's role is summarised in its mission statement: "The NCA aims to audit and improve the regularity, efficiency, effectiveness and integrity with which the state and its associated bodies operate. It also audits compliance with the Netherlands' obligations under international agreements. As part of this process it passes on the results of its audits, as well as its accumulated experience, to the government, to the parliament and to those responsible for the bodies audited. As a rule, this information is also available to the public. It consists of audit findings, opinions and recommendations concerning organisation, management and policy. Another task is to contribute to sound public administration through co-operation and knowledge exchange at home and abroad".

The National Ombudsman

The National Ombudsman investigates whether the government has behaved properly towards members of the public.[13] The institution of National Ombudsman, which tasks are laid down in a specific law, is established in order to give individuals an opportunity to place complaints about the practices of government before an independent and expert body. But citizens should complain at the respective government organisation itself first, otherwise the ombudsman will not treat the complaint. Generally speaking the Ombudsman will investigate a specific complaint to check whether the criteria for proper (government) conduct have been met. His decisions are not legally enforceable, but if he does make a recommendation to a government organisation, this is almost always followed up.

The Ombudsman can also initiate his own investigations (without reacting on received complaints), often leading to a report on a specific government sector, practice or problem. Approximately four to five of these reports are drawn up every year.

Subnational levels of government

Provinces and municipalities

The Netherlands is a decentralised unitary state with three tiers of government. It is divided into 12 provinces[14] and 441 municipalities[15]. Each province and municipality has its own council, elected by popular vote. Their executives are chaired by provincial governors (Queen's commissioners) and mayors, who are appointed by the central government, and who also chair their council. They can be established, dissolved, and their boundaries can be revised by act of the parliament. The Ministry of Interior has overall co-ordinating responsibility for local government affairs.

There are significant differences in size between municipalities. The "big four" cover the four main cities of Amsterdam, Den Haag, Utrecht, and Rotterdam.[16] These interact directly with central government ministries. The Association of Netherlands Municipalities (VNG) speaks on behalf of the smaller municipalities.

Water boards

In addition, there are water boards, which are responsible for water management. The water boards are one of the oldest democratic institutions in the Netherlands. Water management is an important issue as about one quarter of the Netherlands lies below sea level. The boards are public bodies, with executive councils elected for the most part by property owners in their localities. The chair of the executive committee is appointed by the central government.

Powers and responsibilities

Provincial and municipal authorities have important implementation and enforcement (including inspection) functions, especially in physical and environmental planning, and in licensing, based on regulations laid down by central government. Regarding inspections, responsibilities (and execution) are shared between local governments and central government for most areas (for example in the hotel and catering industry 44% of inspections are done by local governments, the rest by central government). Municipalities are also required to implement certain measures laid down by the province to which they belong.

Provinces and municipalities also have limited powers to make their own regulations (bye-laws) on matters that directly affect them, and they may also make additional regulations in areas that have already been regulated at national level. Provincial executives implement a number of central government regulations in joint governance. The Constitution and the Municipal Act set the framework for local rule- making. The General Municipal Ordinance contains most of the local regulation.

Provincial authorities are responsible for environmental management, spatial planning, energy supply, social work, sport and cultural affairs. They also play a co-ordinating and planning role, and supervise the finances of the municipalities.

Municipal authorities are responsible for water supply, traffic, housing, public authority schools, social services, health care, sport, recreation, and culture.

Funding

Provinces and municipalities have two main sources of income: local taxes and charges which amount to some 7% of total income for municipalities,[17] and central government funding. Most of the latter is in the form of ring-fenced special purpose grants. In addition, municipalities receive block grants from the provinces and municipalities funds which they can spend as they see fit. Municipalities draft their budget annually on the basis of the Budget and Accountability Decree for Provinces and Municipalities.

Notes

1. The Kingdom was established in 1814, and was preceded by the Republic of the United Provinces, established in 1648.
2. The Netherlands has a constitution. The counterpart for the entire Kingdom is its charter, which states that the Kingdom is based on the principle of autonomy. In other words, each country is responsible for its own governance.
3. The most recent amendment was in 2002.
4. Ministry of General Affairs, Ministry of Interior and Kingdom Relations, Ministry of Foreign Affairs and Development Co-operation, Ministry of Defence, Ministry of Economic Affairs, Ministry of Finance, Ministry of Justice, Ministry of Agriculture, Nature and Food Quality, Ministry of Education, Culture and Science, Ministry of Social Affairs and Employment, Ministry of Transport, Public Works

and Water Management, Ministry of Health, Welfare and Sport, Ministry of Housing, Spatial Planning and the Environment.

5. General Inspection Service, Labour Inspectorate, Health Care Inspectorate, Inspectorate for Public Order and Safety, Inspectorate of Transport, Public Works and Water Management, Education Inspectorate, State Inspectorate for Cultural Heritage, Food and Consumer Product Safety Authority, Inspectorate of Housing, Spatial Planning and the Environment. There are other types of agency under this category, such as the State Archive Agency.

6. The SER can also issue ordinances setting up commodity boards and marketing boards for groups of companies that perform the same role or are concerned with the same product. It can also set up umbrella commodity boards embracing several smaller boards. Until now, this has only been done for the agricultural sector (the Marketing Board for Dairy Products). The boards can adopt binding regulations in their own policy areas. Some decisions require the prior approval of central government.

7. See *www.houseofrepresentativesnl.*

8. Up to ten parties are regularly represented in government. In the past, very large coalitions made up of four to five parties emerged from elections, which often fell apart, giving rise to minority coalition governments.

9. See also *www.raadvanstate.nl.*

10. See *www.derechtspraak.nl.*

11. The Council of State (for cases relating to the environment, spatial planning, immigration), the *Centrale Raad van Beroep* (for cases relating to the Civil Service Act - *Ambtenarenwet*) and the *College van Beroep voor het Bderijfsleven* (for cases relating to agriculture and other economic sectors).

12. The Court is a « High Council of State » alongside the Council of State, the two houses of the parliament, and the National Ombudsman.

13. See *www.nationaleombudsman.nl.*

14. Groningen, Friesland, Drenthe, Overijssel, Gelderland, Utrecht, North Holland, South Holland, Zeeland, North Brabant, Limburg, Flevoland.

15. As of January 2009.

16. Economic activity is concentrated in the area known as the *Randstad*, the urban belt that includes the country's four main cities.

17. Property tax, court fees, local charges such as dog licences.

Annex B. Key stages in the development of the Netherlands regulatory burden reduction programme

1994 – MDW (Marktwerking, Deregulering en Wetgevingskwaliteit) programme which targeted the better functioning of markets, deregulation and legislative quality. A main aim of the *MDW* programme was the reduction of administrative burdens- to streamline regulations in order to return to "what is strictly necessary". In 1993, it was estimated that the aggregate costs of administrative burdens on companies was more than 2% of GDP.

1998 – Coalition agreement and establishment of the Slechte Committee. A target of reducing costs by 10% was judged to have been met in 1998. The parliament then passed a widely-supported motion to reduce burdens by a further 15%, a target which was integrated into the 1998 coalition agreement. The cabinet set up the Committee for Reduction of Administrative Burdens on Enterprises (the *Slechte* Committee, named after its chairman) to advice on meeting the target. The committee consisted of SME representatives, large enterprises, subnational levels of government, accounting firms, political parties, the European Parliament, and specialists in public administration, organisational consulting, and communication. Ministries were involved through a steering group.

1999 – Report of the Slechte Committee. The committee marked a turning point in that it decided to focus solely on costs imposed on enterprises, excluding other target groups. It distinguished between three types of cost: the costs of compliance for enterprises; the costs of law enforcement by public authorities; and the costs of information enterprises had to supply to make law enforcement possible. It recommended that the third category should be the sole focus for reduction. The committee presented 60 projects for reducing this type of burden. It built its approach on two pillars: re-use of information already provided by enterprises to public authorities, and use of ICT mechanisms. The committee also proposed a systematic and independent monitoring and measurement of administrative burdens. Most of the committee's recommendations were accepted by the cabinet and the parliament.

This narrow focus was subsequently maintained, with a view to depoliticising the issue of burden reduction, as the objectives of individual regulations would not be discussed, nor the balance between benefits and costs. The focus was on the "general interest" issue of reducing administrative costs while maintaining the essence of the regulation. In other words: not less regulation, but smarter regulation.

2001 – Establishment of ACTAL. In 2001, the cabinet established an Advisory Board on Administrative Burdens (ACTAL), to support the government's work on the basis of the recommendations of the Committee

Prior to the 2003 elections, administrative burdens were judged to have been reduced by 7% compared with 1994. As the burdens following from new legislation were not yet systematically assessed at this stage, this percentage is the gross reduction. The net reduction would be smaller due to the introduction of new burdens in new regulations over the period.

2003-07 – Consolidation of the Dutch model. The period following the 2003 election saw the consolidation and refinement of the Dutch model. Its main features were the establishment of a baseline measurement of burdens against which progress could be assessed, a quantified reduction target, a link to the budget cycle, and a strong supporting institutional structure made up of a central monitoring and co-ordinating government unit flanked by an independent advisory body (ACTAL). The programme had strong political support. Administrative burdens were defined as "the costs to the businesses of complying with the information obligations resulting from government-imposed legislation and regulations".

In 2003 the government set the objective of reducing burdens by 25% before the end of 2007, relative to a 2003 baseline measurement, which was estimated at EUR 16.4 billion (3.6% of GDP). The baseline showed the distribution of burdens across ministries.[1] The baseline also showed the distribution of burdens on individual regulations. It also showed that ten laws accounted for more than half of the total burden.[2]

Information obligations were divided into three categories according to their origin:

- Administrative burdens imposed and implemented at international level – accounting for more than 40% of the total burden.
- Administrative burdens imposed at international level, implemented at national level – accounting for approximately 10% of the total burden.
- Administrative burdens imposed and implemented at national level – accounting for more than 40% of the total burden.

Distribution of burdens across the three categories varied by ministry, with some ministries having almost purely national legislation, others mainly international regulation, and others a mix of the three categories.

2003 – First package of initiatives. The first package of initiatives to reduce the burdens was based on this measurement and on inventories compiled by the nine participating ministries. It was decided not to impose the same reduction targets on all ministries, but rather to set for each ministry a total gross reduction target. The reductions, which varied from 10% (Ministry of Health) to 31% (Ministry of Environment), added up to a total reduction of 18%. Most of the reductions were scheduled to materialise in the years 2006 and 2007, towards the end of the period, as many of the initiatives had to be implemented by a lengthy legislation process and/or the development of ICT solutions.

2005 - Second package of initiatives. A second package followed in 2005, raising the overall burden reduction target from 18% to 25% (to meet the original target set in 2003). Significantly, the target was also made a net target, by setting ceilings for each ministry (now ten ministries), meaning that any new burdens arising from new regulations had to be cancelled out by a corresponding removal of burdens from existing regulations.[3]

Current approach 2007-11

Less

25% lower administrative burden for business

The measures in the reduction plans of the individual ministries will make it possible to achieve the cabinet's objective of a 25% net reduction in administrative burden by 2011. The reference point is the administrative burden as of 1 March 2007 as measured in the zero base measurement of administrative burden for business in 2007. The results of the zero base measurement were reported to the parliament in the progress report of May 2008. The programme also reaches out to the local levels of government (which have agreed to play their part in the reduction), and links up with the programme for further reform of inspections and enforcement. It includes further initiatives to streamline licensing, based on the *lex silencio* (silence is consent) principle.

Lower compliance costs

The progress report of May 2008 named 30 fields in which businesses find the compliance costs disproportionately high. Seven pilot projects have since been completed and they have shown that the measurement method used is valid and practicable. The actual measurement of the problems put forward by businesses in the other 23 fields have been completed end of February 2009.

The concrete reduction proposals will be charted in the spring of 2009. These proposals will form the foundation for the degree (percentage) of reduction in compliance costs in the priority fields in the next progress report (spring 2009).

Lower supervisory costs

In the 19 fields in which supervisory costs were measured, a 25% reduction will be achieved through measures such as ensuring that SME enterprises in those fields are inspected twice a year at most. This means a further reduction of another EUR 25 million on top of the 25% reduction in administrative burden. Surely equally important from the point of view of businesses is that this will be coupled with a qualitative improvement of services by the inspectorates.

Lower costs in relation to subsidies

Also a subsidy framework is being developed which will simplify all national government subsidies and ensure that management and implementation costs are kept low. All subsidy schemes for businesses will be reviewed on the basis of this framework during the present cabinet's term in office.

Simpler

More transparent

Businesses must be able to find up-to-date and comprehensible information that applies to them in a quick and simple manner. The cabinet wants to achieve this with the help of *Antwoordvoorbedrijven.nl*. The present number of visitors (960 000 per year) is to increase to 1.5 million in 2011. By then, 62 "regulatory navigators" are to be operational. This year there are 32.

More predictable

By more predictable, the cabinet means that any changes in legislation will only take effect on two dates in a year and that these changes will be announced well ahead of time in understandable language. The target in this area is for all ministries to use the system of common commencement dates by 2011.

Faster

Faster decision making is in part made possible by a broad application of *lex silencio.* In 2007, there were 21 licensing systems that worked with *lex silencio.* By 2011, the Cabinet wants to see this 2007 figure of the number of licensing systems working with *lex silencio* doubled.

Better service

The top ten implementing organisations named in the zero base measurement of administrative burden that play an important role in the perceived regulatory burden for business must meet minimum quality requirements for services by 2011. On the one hand, these organisations translate legislation and regulations into concrete policy rules or forms and procedures. They can therefore influence the perceived administrative burden. On the other hand, they are the organisations with direct contacts with business. These contacts affect the irritation or satisfaction with information obligations.

The top ten also includes the municipalities. With regard to the municipalities, by the end of its term of office the Cabinet wants to see that:

- at least 200 municipalities;
- which together accommodate at least half of all businesses established in the Netherlands;
- periodically measure the quality of their services; and
- work at least in accordance with the minimum standards.

Tangible

To be able to know how all these actions influence regulatory burdens, every spring the cabinet will measure to what extent businesses are irritated by regulatory burden. In the "perception monitor", several statements about regulatory burden are presented to businesses. A number of these statements are closely related to the previously mentioned priorities of the programme. The cabinet wants to see the perception of businesses develop in a positive sense on these points.

The cabinet also wants to see businesses give seven out of ten points to the quality of services provided by both municipalities and implementing organisations as charted in the context of the perception monitor.

	Aspect	Objective 2011
LESS	Administrative Burden	-25% net
	Compliance costs	Percentage of extraneous costs to business in 30 high-priority fields, to be determined after measurement. Outcomes in progress report of spring 2009.
	Supervisory burden for 19 domains due to inspections by the national government	-25%
	Subsidies	100% of national government subsidies for businesses are to entail low management and implementation costs
SIMPLER	More predictable	Common commencement dates take effect in all ministries
	More transparent	▪ Antwoordvoorbedrijven.nl: 1.5m visitors per year ▪ Regulatory navigators for 62 industries
	Faster	Doubling the number of licensing systems that work with *Lex Silencio* compared to 2007
	Better service	▪ System of standards for services must be used by 200 municipalities ▪ The same for the top 10 implementing bodies
TANGIBLE	Predictability	15% more businesses say they are not irritated by continually changing legislation and rules
	Information obligations	25% more businesses say they have very little irritation from unnecessary information obligations
	Supervision	15% more businesses say they have very little irritation from strict requirements of supervisory bodies
	Lower costs to comply with regulations	25% more businesses say they have very little irritation from high costs to comply with rules.

Source: 2007 OECD report, and Netherlands government.

Notes

1. Ministry of Finance (EUR 4.32 billion), Ministry of Health (EUR 3.20 billion), Ministry of Social Affairs (EUR 2.53 billion), Ministry of Justice (EUR 2.51 billion), Ministry of the Environment (EUR 1.68 billion), Ministry of Transport (EUR 1.04 billion), Ministry of Economic Affairs (EUR 0.67 billion), Ministry of Agriculture (EUR 0.43 billion), Ministry of Education (EUR 0.02 billion).

2. Annual Accounts Act Turnover Tax Act, Commodities Act, Environmental Management Act, Wages and Salaries Tax Act, Compulsory Health Insurance Act, Social Security (Co-ordination) Act, Income Tax Act, Prices Act, Working Conditions Act.

3. Ten initiatives would account for the largest burden reductions: Annual accounts x 2, Annual pay statement x 2, Turnover tax, Financial information leaflet, Occupational Health and Safety, Manure legislation, Annual Accounts.

OECD PUBLISHING, 2, rue André-Pascal, 75775 PARIS CEDEX 16
PRINTED IN FRANCE
(42 2010 13 1 P) ISBN 978-92-64-08451-3 – No. 57321 2010